WHAT NOW?

How Teen Therapeutic Programs Could Save Your Troubled Child

© 2007 Paul Wesley Case, Psy.D

Catalog in Publication data is available.

ISBN-13: 978-1-93431-430-2

Published by Common Thread Media, 101 Forrest Crossing Boulevard, Suite 100
Franklin, Tennessee, 37064

First printing 2007

Printed in the United States of America
10 9 8 7 6 5 4 3 2 1

Managing Editor: Melany Klinck
Interior and cover design: Marc Pewitt

What Now? is available for purchase in bulk quantities. Visit **www.commonthreadmedia.com**.

WHAT NOW?

How Teen Therapeutic Programs Could Save Your Troubled Child

Dr. PAUL CASE

with foreword by John A. McKinnon, MD

COMMON THREAD MEDIA

Franklin, Tennessee

TABLE OF CONTENTS

Acknowledgements

They say it takes a village to raise a child. It also takes a village to write and publish a book. My "village" has included hundreds of families with whom I have worked over the years. They have taught me many things about both being an adolescent and parenting an adolescent in contemporary society. My village has also included a number of colleagues who are involved in providing care for struggling teens. I cannot list them all, of course, but I am indebted to them for all the things that they have taught me, whether in formal settings or in casual conversations. I am especially grateful to those of my colleagues who have recognized the intense challenges facing today's parents of children and adolescents, not the least of which are the serious limitations of existing treatment options for teens who are struggling to be successful in mainstream America. Many of these colleagues have had the vision to think outside of the box and create viable therapeutic options that promote teen development rather than simply reducing symptoms.

I want to mention a few of them who have had a particular impact on my thinking about how to work effectively with struggling teens. Dr. John McKinnon and Dr. John Santa are the founders of Montana Academy, a therapeutic boarding school located outside of Kalispell, Montana. I had the great opportunity to work alongside them while I served as a Clinical Supervisor at Montana Academy. Dr. McKinnon and Dr. Santa have preserved a way of understanding and treating adolescent problems that emphasizes the need for teens to develop maturity in their lives and relationships within the context of significant and attuned relationships with adults and peers. My thinking about how to work effectively with adolescents has been significantly influenced by the years that I spent with them. Though I have made every effort to acknowledge their ideas throughout this book, I am certain that their influence resonates in my own approach to understanding and treating adolescent problems. I am especially grateful to Dr. McKinnon for reading drafts of this manuscript and offering guidance along the way, and for contributing the foreword to this book.

I want to thank my colleagues at Second Nature Blue Ridge Wilderness Program, who challenge and inspire me to continually grow and develop in my work with adolescents and their families. I am particularly grateful to Kathy Donovan, LCSW, Lu Vaughn, LPC, and Dawn Huff, who read drafts of this manuscript and offered helpful suggestions. I am also grateful to Dan McDougal, who was supportive and encouraging as I poured my time and energy into writing this book.

I am grateful to Dr. Douglas Norfleet and the staff at Common Thread Media for their commitment and professionalism in getting this book to press. I am especially grateful to Melany Klinck, who served as editor for this book. Melany helped make this book more user-friendly and compelling for readers who are looking for help in this process but do not want to be bogged down by theoretical and academic musings.

I am grateful to Roger Waynick, who saw a need for a book like this to be available to the many parents in crisis with their adolescents. Roger has been patient and steadfast in his desire to provide such a resource for parents.

Finally, I am grateful to my friends and family for their support, encouragement, and patience with me in the writing process. I am especially grateful to Hampton Shive and Alan Daigre, who have been available companions throughout this project and throughout two decades of life projects. And Kathleen Mercer has been a true source of encouragement and support, willing to read numerous versions of this manuscript and share her wisdom with me all along the way.

Thanks to all of you!

Paul Wesley Case, Psy.D.
November 6, 2007

Foreword

By John A. McKinnon, MD
CEO, Montana Academy

Dr. Paul Case has written an engaging book for worried parents of troubled and troubling teenagers. He writes of adolescent sons and daughters who are failing across the board at the usual tasks of adolescence—at school, at home, among peers, and unhappily closeted in their own bedrooms.

Troubled teenagers have always been with us. After 40 years I can picture faces of flailing classmates who stopped trying in math class and dropped out. I still can hear the whispered gossip about a girl who had "gone all the way" in the back of a Buick, about her precocious pregnancy and abrupt visit to Aunt Audrey in Amarillo. I still can recall the first time at a school dance that I saw a six-pack of beer under the open trunk lid of a raked Pontiac. And I can recall my grief, at 14, when a favorite cheerleader took a fatal overdose of aspirin, and how appalled I felt when a spastic boy in my civics class, humiliated in the lunch line by an oblivious fullback, hung himself in his bedroom.

Teen troubles have always been with us, but the numbers certainly appear to be larger today. Teen troubles are routinely in the news, the subjects of public debate. Contemporary teenagers fail standard tests and drop out of school so frequently that senators worry about the teenaged "child left behind." In our contemporary culture, oral sex and intercourse among adolescents have become so commonplace that, in this age of "hooking up," the locker-room gossip of my adolescent pals sounds prissy and antique. Abortion, a word we did not say aloud in polite company when I was a teenager, is today the unseemly topic of rancorous political argument. Why? Because in our culture, promiscuous teenagers in urban and suburban neighborhoods—where cocaine has become a party drug and bourgeois children are snorting heroine—often produce pregnancies. Who can even recall anymore a time when a can of Pabst Blue Ribbon at a school dance was considered *risqué*?

As contemporary culture has become more conducive to adolescent problems and the cohort of troubled young people has enlarged, effective psychiatric treatment has become less available. For many troubled teenagers, medications fail to address the right problems—greatly improving symptoms some of the time, but not catching and turning around an adolescent nosedive. Weekly outpatient psychotherapy does not suffice for all troubled sons and daughters, and it may be impossible to persuade a recalcitrant teenager to cooperate. In short, outpatient interventions cannot provide the sustained and intensive remedies that ever greater numbers of sons and daughters need. No doubt sensible to the economic threat this rising need entails, insurance companies exclude adolescent residential treatment from their policies. For those without private resources, sustained residential treatment has always been unavailable except to those chronically delinquent youth who are already so deeply addicted and psychologically damaged that they are resistant and impervious to short-term public rehabilitation facilities. Criminal "adjudicated" teenagers are a distinct population from the more privileged teenagers Dr. Case describes.[1]

Yet when these two distinctive groups are summed, the number of troubled American teenagers needing sustained residential treatment is large indeed. Dr. John Santa, then president of the National Association of Therapeutic Schools and Programs (NATSAP), pointed out in 2007:

[M]ost children end up in private residential treatment only after they have failed in numerous attempts in outpatient and community-based settings. Most come from private paying families who have tried numerous interventions with various types of therapy and medication. Private residential placement is attempted only after all else has failed. And yet there were more than 18,000 young people enrolled in [private residential] programs during 2005. If we add to this the number of adolescents in public sector residential programs, the correctional system—and those wandering the streets—the number grows into hundreds of thousands, if not millions.[2]

Even as scarce public-sector beds have been restricted to teenagers so damaged that they are unlikely to respond in any definitive way to short-term residential treatment, conventional private psychiatric hospital programs and residential treatment centers have atrophied—*not* because contemporary families and their doctors have no use for them, but because insurance "managed care" companies refuse to "authorize" their use. In recent years, conventional psychiatric (medical) inpatient and residential beds have simply been "managed" out of existence.

However, the need for residential care—if you ask responsible parents—has not been "managed" away. Insurance companies have only succeeded in ducking the duty to pay for that needed care. As a result, parents with troubled teenagers have had to look elsewhere for help, if they could pay for that help themselves, without insurance reimbursement.

In this barren psychiatric wasteland, created largely by the success of medical insurance companies in preventing sustained residential treatment for teenagers, there has arisen, like mushrooms after a forest fire, a large number and substantial variety of "alternative" (non-medical) treatment programs for troubled youth. In 1990 there were about 50 alternative "wilderness" and "emotional growth" programs in the nation, according to the National Association of Therapeutic Schools and Programs (NATSAP), which did not exist then. Ten years later in 2000, when NATSAP was just getting organized, there were about 100 such programs. Only seven years after that, the number of programs that had become dues-paying members of NATSAP, and subscribed to its published Code of Ethics and Practice Guidelines, had nearly reached 200.

Dr. Case has written a friendly, informative introduction to this "alternative" world. He knows what he's talking about, but not because Paul Case personally has catalogued every school and program in America. (To tap into that kind of travel-weary, encyclopedic knowledge, parents must consult another kind of expert—see below). Rather, Dr. Case is an experienced clinician, who has worked for years in this leafy alternative mundo. He understands with a clinical *savoir faire* the essential treatment virtues of two innovative institutions that have arisen within this alternative world: the *wilderness* program and the *residential therapeutic school*.

Dr. Case knows how these programs work, how they have come to be structured and staffed, and how they help troubled teenagers to get "better." He knows how parents feel, how they respond to their children's troubles (sometimes well, and sometimes not very well) under the enormous strain they endure when their son's or a daughter's life goes awry. He explains how treatment works in the rugged outdoor treks we call "wilderness" treatment. And he explains how the structure and culture of a good therapeutic boarding school influence failing and troubled teenagers, so as to push them to change and to become less troubled. He knows about "experiential" treatment and education that takes place, these days, far from the antiseptic corridors of a locked psychiatric hospital. Dr. Case knows what he is talking about, because he has worked for years in these two new kinds of non-medical institutions.

For some years now Dr. Case has been a field therapist at Second Nature, one of the nation's larger and most competent "wilderness" programs. Working in the wilds of the southeast with unhappy teenagers, who have been obliged by their parents to hike long trails under heavy packs and to build shelters to camp and cook in the wild, he became skilled at the "experiential" approach to psychotherapy. He learned to conduct group and individual therapy in the outback, where teenagers struggle to accomplish feats of endurance and to acquire skills they can immediately use—to sleep in a dry bag, to eat a hot dinner—and so build the basis for legitimate self-esteem. In the field, weather and terrain produce "natural consequences" for a flawed approach to life, and Dr. Case is there with these teenagers, when they became tired, scared and homesick, ready to rethink wasted privileges and empty days, to reconsider their unhappy parents and siblings. Under a starry night sky, far from suburban and city lights, he helps narcissistic teenagers contemplate the larger purposes of their lives—to consider how the future might be different—and to get ready to start anew at a residential therapeutic school.

Prior to his work in the wild, Dr. Case worked for some years as a therapist and clinical supervisor at Montana Academy, which is a residential therapeutic school. There we became colleagues and friends. On Montana Academy's ranch campus, located west of Glacier Park in northern Montana, he took care of a group of 10 teenaged boys who, prior to enrollment, had been failing in school (although they were bright); who had disrupted their families and frightened their parents (although these were fundamentally kind, non-malicious young people); who had been sliding down the adolescent social register, hanging around with more and more disreputable friends (if they still had any friends at all); and who had become unhappy (ashamed, guilty, hurt, worried, angry) even alone in their own bedrooms, where they had been cutting themselves, drinking or taking drugs, distracting themselves with video games or pornography, or contemplating suicide. In those years on the ranch, Dr. Case presided over these boys for 14-20 months as they attended a demanding prep school, worked in the kitchen or shop, and lived and played with other boys on a ranch 40 miles from the nearest town. He also presided over weekend activities with staff, team leaders, a consulting psychiatrist and teacher, who constituted the team who implemented the treatment plan that he defined and coordinated. In those years he proved to be a sensitive, gifted therapist, who mastered the unique developmental model of treatment at Montana Academy.

Talking with parents about troubled sons and daughters, then, comes naturally to Paul Case. He addresses his book in a friendly, informal fashion to "you." His accessible explanations—of the debacle that brings a troubled family to a crisis; of the escort to wilderness; of the wilderness interventions, which communicate an unmistakable parental determination that the debacle will not continue; of a sustained residential therapeutic school experience, which can bring a lasting change in a teenager's emerging psychology; and of the homecoming—are all redolent with his personal experience with teenagers and parents, whether at home, in the field, at base camp, or in residence at a therapeutic ranch school. From experience he can speak directly to anguished parents about the angst they experience when their children fail, globally and repeatedly, and when outpatient psychological and psychiatric interventions fail them both.

Dr. Case explains the role of educational consultants, who, over the past few decades, have assumed a new professional role in our society and a critical place in the alternative treatment world. Educational consultants get paid to know in detail (having been there) about the available programs and schools across the nation and even off-shore; they consult with parents about their children, so as to advise parents which wilderness, emotional growth program, residential treatment center or therapeutic school best fits a teen-ager's particular academic, emotional and social needs. The best available programs are usually national in their reach. They accept for enrollment troubled campers or students from across the county, even from other countries. Although some inexperienced clinicians feel indignant when parents consult educational consultants, when they break off outpatient therapy that has produced no tangible results, or when parents consider a distant alternative placement, the better-informed and more experienced clinicians, who have followed a free-falling teenager through the radical changes that can occur during residential placement in "alternative" programs and school, come to value this useful consultation.

For such informed advice safely opens up that alternative world to young patients and their families. It is all but impossible for a busy clinician to learn enough about faraway programs to make an informed referral, even when it has become obvious that an outpatient strategy is not resolving a teenager's global problems. I did not know about these programs when I used to run an office practice. How could I have known? How can any busy clinician, who has no time to investigate, come to know for sure what educational consultants make it their business to learn? It is obvious to me that those noisy clinicians who recently have railed about the very idea that parents should send a disturbed, out-of-control teenager away from home—and far from their outpatient offices, presumably—have not visited reputable and competent programs and schools. They cannot have studied the relevant data.[3] Nor can they have discussed the matter with well-educated parents of teenaged children who were at high risk for academic self-destruction, addiction, criminal sanctions or psychiatric morbidity, including suicide. They cannot have discussed these problems with assiduous parents whose troubled teenagers had rendered their homes uninhabitable—and already had failed repeatedly in outpatient therapies in the hands of competent psychiatrists and psychologists.

To know in detail about those alternative interventions, to sort the intelligent from the inane, takes a visit and time to interview key professional staff, to meet campers or students, and to inspect the facility or campus. It also takes sufficient experience to ask probing questions and to check the answers. This being so, skilled contemporary clinicians who wish to make available to their patients and their families the best treatment available, will work regularly with competent, experienced, well-traveled educational consultants.

As Paul Case knows, a wilderness or residential treatment recommendation is jarring for parents, whether it comes from a seasoned clinician or experienced educational consultant, or whether parents have come to this painful conclusion on their own. For parents who have jobs to do, careers to maintain, other children to care for, and who do not enjoy unlimited financial resources, this decision can be disruptive, even earth-shaking. For a parent to endure a confrontation with an angry teenager and then to send an unhappy daughter or son far away is a wrenching experience. There is always grief in it. I have not yet encountered a loving parent who has made this decision without suffering.

Parents who face this kind of momentous decision will value Dr. Case's expert advice and should find his experience reassuring. In my own experience with young people arriving from successful wilderness interventions and successfully participating in the therapeutic and academic program at Montana Academy, the outcome is almost invariably positive—both for failing, flailing teenagers and for their families. Parents almost always find it a relief to put a stop to a chaotic, out-of-control, risky debacle, to find competent help, to settle all the members of the family down, and to get to work, all together, to create the psychological and family bases for a son or daughter to get back to academics, to make and keep worthy friends, and to recover legitimate self-respect. Very often, in our experience, the results are salutary.

On the other hand, state governments have been slow to supervise therapeutic programs. When we opened in 1997 we tried to find a state agency (Health and Human Services or Department of Labor) to license us. We were dumbfounded to discover that no state agency in Helena (other than the state fire marshal) had any jurisdiction over a new school and residential therapeutic program. They were not even curious. Moreover, in the decade since its inception, no state official has ever visited Montana Academy, although, because we are proud of what we have created, we have invited state bureaucrats, legislators and the governor.

This lack of oversight is worrisome. Just consider that state medical boards report every year on the disciplinary actions they have taken against physicians found to be addled, addicted, irresponsible or incompetent. Consider that hospitals are regularly inspected—not without reason. Moreover, aside from miscreants, when it comes to children and teenagers, the world teems with well-meaning fools, some of them apt to start a "program." Yet regulation is still lacking.

For these reasons the best schools and programs want deft and intelligent regulation, knowing all the while that inept, clumsy regulation could destroy what parents have had to come so far to find. Like other physicians who welcome state medical board oversight of the profession, I am anxious that children be cared for properly and also concerned that wretched programs and scandal not give the entire panoply of alternative programs for teenagers a bad reputation. Along with our responsible colleagues, we ourselves have asked for sensible regulation and are lobbying for it. Yet as I write—although Montana Academy has seven certified teachers and has long enjoyed academic accreditation from the Northwest Association of Schools and Colleges; although it has eight doctorate-level psychologists and two board-certified psychiatrists on campus; and although the academy has achieved clinical accreditation from the Joint Commission on Accreditation of Healthcare Organizations (JCAHO)—there is not as yet a licensure or inspection process in place in Montana, and no state official has crossed our cattle-guard to see what we are doing.

Here is my point: Choosing a wilderness program or therapeutic school can be difficult, if not perilous. Local clinicians usually cannot know which program to recommend and may resist the very idea of residential care. State regulation cannot always be relied upon. And yet the best alternative programs—as parents and consultants who have done the due diligence regularly tell me—also provide the best residential treatment available. As a result of managed care's squeeze on conventional psychiatric programs, there _is_ nothing else as high quality, and nowhere else for desperate parents to go. This reality makes the opinion of competent educational consultants valuable, even though that advice may be expensive. It takes many months of travel and work to accumulate the knowledge which makes their advice sound.

This is why you may find Dr. Case's book worth its weight in gold. For he explains here what a clinical nugget ought to look like and what effective treatment and academic support should accomplish. He explains what parents ought to search for and, with a little good advice and some diligent homework, can hope to find. And I think it will be impossible after reading his book to still imagine that clinical ore will be easy to discern by calling an 800 marketing telephone number or panning the classified ads in *Sunset* magazine.

To prepare parents for what they may face, Dr. Case teaches a little about adolescent psychology, recounting various theories (including my own[4]) as to what goes wrong in adolescence. Then, in a practical way, he walks parents through a wilderness program, a therapeutic school experience, and the demands such experiences place upon the adults who hover over this sustained effort. He describes the restoration of sound parent-child relationships, discusses drug and alcohol treatment, sorts out psychiatric symptoms and problems. He urges parents to take the opportunity, which a teenager's crisis affords them, to consider their own lives, their marriages, their own experiences with their parents, and to ask themselves what contributions they may have made to their son's or daughter's problems. This adult participation is critical, even if painful. For in my experience, teenagers rarely resolve all their emotional difficulties unilaterally.

Here I am hinting at the essential problem that parents, clinicians and teenagers must solve together. A teenager may well suffer from a vulnerability to become depressed under stress, or he may struggle to stay focused on the task at hand in the classroom. No argument. But if a "chemical imbalance" were the simple explanation for teenagers' troubles, then pharmacology would turn out to be a simple, promptly effective solution to all that ails them. However, by the time anyone thinks a residential placement may be worth talking about, a teenager's underlying problem is much more than a symptom that simply requires a pill for relief.

For what usually is at issue whenever teenagers begin to flounder and fail across the spectrum of typical adolescent tasks—at school, at home, among peers—is development itself. Whatever the obstacle (e.g., ADHD, a wrenching parental divorce, or sexual trauma) the resulting disruption in psychological development leaves a teenager relatively *immature*. When this happens, it is necessary, but not sufficient, to remove the obstacle. What also has to happen—even after a trauma has been treated with psychotherapy, even after a depression has lifted with proper medication, even after a learning eccentricity has been tutored and circumvented— is to catch up, to grow up, to get past the flawed approach that made a bright boy or girl fail all the challenges of a modern adolescence.

The remedy, then, for teenagers who have failed repeatedly, globally, is the removal of obstacles from their path, followed by a firm push in the direction of maturation. When this two-step treatment is successful, over time a teenager's symptoms abate, academic and social functioning improve, and kids recover self-esteem and morale. They become willing to try again. Once this happens, the whole family's equilibrium can be re-stored, too. Parent and child can renegotiate their relationship. And when such a young person gets it together in this way, she/he can go off to prep school or college and get on with growing up.

It is because these true therapeutic goals are so global and ambitious, so far beyond mere symptom relief, that they require a "time-out" from the flux of modern culture, so that teenagers themselves, with their parents joining in, can address these developmental problems. The best of the wilderness treks and therapeutic residential schools are shaped to these ends. They are truly inventive, and they provide a treatment that fosters the recovery of developmental momentum. As I have suggested, outpatient treatment may well help, but often it simply cannot effectively offer a definitive time-out, nor provide a sufficient hiatus, or sober respite, for removing obstacles or prodding maturation. And pharmacology, as valuable as it can be in shrinking emotional obstacles, has little efficacy in prodding an immature child to grow up.

Most parents do not expect ever to have to endure these trials with their child. When they must do so, however, they often find that shame or guilt makes it difficult to talk about these struggles, even with friends, friendly neighbors or close family. In this sad and worried time, Paul Case provides a calm, friendly, expert voice, which parents will find a relief to hear.

1. Behrens, Ellen and Satterfield, Kristin (in press). "Longitudinal Family and Academic Outcomes in Residential Programs: How Students Function in Two Important Areas of their Lives," *Journal of Therapeutic Schools and Programs*, 2007.

2. Santa, John (2007) "Residential Treatment and the Missing Axis," an address to the National Association of Therapeutic Schools and Programs (NATSAP), San Diego, February 2007. To be published in the *Journal of Therapeutic Schools and Programs* (in press).

3. Behrens, Ellen and Satterfield, Kristin (2007) "A Multi-Center, Longitudinal Study of Youth Outcomes in Private Residential Treatment Programs," paper presented at the Conference of the Independent Educational Consultants Association, Boston, MA, April 27, 2007.

To my knowledge this is the *only* large-scale, multi-center study of treatment outcomes in this specifically defined private residential treatment population. Summarizing their results, the investigators concluded: "Based on this study, it appears that psychological, social, and familial outcomes for youth treated in private residential treatment are positive and lasting."

4. McKinnon, John (2008) *An Unchanged Mind: The Problem of Immaturity in Adolescence*, Lantern Books (www.lanternbooks.com), New York, in press.

Families in Crisis

Jason and Leah sat facing me on the dark leather sofa in my office. They were here to tell me about their daughter, Sylvia, a 15-year-old who was becoming increasingly difficult to manage. Leah described in detail Sylvia's history, how as a younger child, she had been so full of joy and energy, a favorite among her teachers and her peers. She had a great sense of humor, though lately her jokes were laced with sarcasm and cruelty, particularly towards her parents. In middle school, Sylvia's straight-A average started to dip, and now, halfway through her sophomore year in high school, she was on the verge of failing two classes. Jason and Leah had enlisted the help of tutors and had her evaluated to see if she had a learning disability. Testing indicated that Sylvia had a slower than expected processing speed, but it was not significant enough to warrant the diagnosis of a learning disability. The evaluator suggested that she seemed depressed and recommended weekly therapy. The therapy, however, did not help.

Though Sylvia's counselor believed she was appropriately working on issues of identity and parental expectations for her behavior, Jason and Leah were beginning to feel that they were losing their daughter. Sylvia's interactions with her parents were unpredictable, but most often focused on manipulating them to give her more freedom. She spent hours at her computer instant messaging her friends or text messaging them from her cell phone instead of doing homework or helping out around the house. Because Leah was the primary disciplinarian in the household, conflicts between her and Sylvia were reaching an unbearable threshold. In the midst of an argument, Sylvia would say horrible things to Leah, things Leah could never even imagine saying to her own mother. But Sylvia did not seem remorseful unless she needed something from Leah, when she feigned remorse convincingly.

Then, one week ago, Leah went to check on Sylvia before going to bed. She found the bedroom window cracked open and Sylvia gone. On Sylvia's computer screen was an instant message from someone Leah did not know inviting Sylvia to go get high. When Sylvia returned through the bedroom window several hours later, she found her frantic parents waiting for her. Within minutes, Sylvia was screaming at her parents to keep out of her bedroom and her life!

Jason and Leah knew they had to take action. The next day they met with an educational consultant referred to them by a friend. The consultant listened to their story and recommended they send Sylvia to a therapeutic wilderness program. By the time they arrived at my office, they had gotten over the initial shock of being advised to consider what seemed like a drastic intervention. Still, they had reservations about this course of action and wanted some assurances that it could help. As I listened to their story, I sensed their desperation and concern, and commented on how difficult this decision must be. Jason quickly responded: "The decision to do this is really not that difficult. We know it has to be done. What is so difficult about this is the feeling that we have failed as parents—that we are not able to do what needs to be done for her, and that the best solution is to send her away . . . from us!"

Each year, thousands of parents are in crisis with their adolescent children. These crises go beyond the expected turmoil of adolescence, beyond occasional acting out and pushing of boundaries. These adolescents are more moody and irritable than many of their peers. They exceed the acceptable limits of teenage exploration and begin to form self-destructive patterns. They are described as impulsive, as acting without thought of the consequences of their behavior. They are self-absorbed, acting as if they are entitled to get whatever they want and get it now, and they do not accept "no" in answer to their demands. What's more, these teens seem oblivious to how their behavior impacts others, especially those closest to them. They accept no responsibility for the negative consequences of their decisions. Instead, they blame others, mostly their parents, and heap mountains of guilt upon their shoulders for doing a terrible job of parenting.

For parents of these teens, the crises are persistent, intense and scary. They watch their teenaged sons and daughters make one poor decision after another. Despite the lectures and limits, their kids sink deeper and deeper into a hole of trouble. They hang out with trouble-makers or "druggies," or they isolate themselves and don't hang out with anyone at all. They become more and more withdrawn into the Internet or the iPod or video games. They lead sneaky, secretive lives, and, when confronted, they lie without blinking an eye. They engage in risky, self-destructive behaviors. They steal money from their parents and siblings, or hurt themselves or others in an attempt to cope with how out-of-control they are feeling. One by one, the negative consequences pile up: failure in school, drug and alcohol abuse, run-ins with the legal system, social alienation, pregnancy, suicide attempts, and, all too often, even suicide.

Contrary to popular assumptions, the parents of troubled teens typically are not bad parents. They are often educated, hard-working, and successful. They are loving parents, most of them, who genuinely care about their kids and want them to be successful in whatever they do. Many of these parents have read the available books on parenting and attended parenting seminars. They have been diligent in seeking solutions to the problems they are encountering with their children. Some have rallied school officials to develop individualized education plans for their sons or daughters. Others have been to see therapists and implemented behavioral contingency programs. They have tried various medications to help their teenagers improve their attention spans and control their erratic moods. Most of the parents have imposed limits and suffered through demoralizing power struggles. They have restricted Internet time and text messaging, and they have invested in new hobbies and activities for their kids. Some have even picked up and moved to new cities to try to give their kids a fresh start. A few have promised a car, a horse, or other rewards, if only the kids will do their best in school and stay out of trouble.

Despite these efforts, their kids continue in a downward spiral that exhausts resources and defies all attempts to help. These parents ultimately find themselves with limited options and difficult choices. For many, one recommended treatment option is to place their child in a therapeutic wilderness program or a therapeutic boarding school. Along with this recommendation, these parents are advised that their children may need to be in an out-of-home placement for a year or more, during which time their contact with their children will be seriously restricted and intruded upon by therapists and program structure. For some, choosing this option will mark an earlier than expected end to having their child live at home. For all, it will come at enormous financial and emotional cost.

This book is written for the parents of these kids. In my work over the years as a psychologist in outpatient settings, at a therapeutic boarding school, and more recently, at a wilderness therapy program, I have listened to the anguish in parents' voices as they have endured this process. Often, they are riddled with guilt and doubt, and they feel like they are failures as parents. They are confused about what to do, though certainly willing to do whatever is necessary to provide their sons and daughters with the help they need. But, disillusioned by the failure of outpatient therapy, psychiatric medications, tutors, and strong parental limits to really help their kids, they are skeptical and desperate. They feel helpless, hopeless and exhausted. Most of all, they feel alone.

Perhaps if you are reading this, you are one of these parents. Maybe you have already made the difficult decision to send your child to a wilderness program or a residential therapeutic school. Or maybe you are just beginning to consider these options, aware that things are out of control with your teenager, but hesitant to take such drastic measures. Wherever you are in this process, and it most certainly is a process, this book will provide you with:

- **Understanding** of why your teenagers are struggling;
- **Explanations** of how a therapeutic school or program can address the problems of your teenager;
- **Validation** for the emotions you are experiencing;
- **Suggestions** for what you can work on while your child is away;
- **Hope** for how you can make this a transformational process for your children as well as for yourself.

In the following pages, you'll find many stories from families like yours. These are all drawn from my actual case material. I have disguised any identifying information to maintain the confidentiality of those I have

Therapeutic Programs ≠ Boot Camps

What comes to mind for many people when they hear the phrase *wilderness program* or *therapeutic boarding school* is a teen boot camp or military school. The therapeutic schools and programs that I am speaking about are *not* boot camps. They are programs that value humane, evidence-based treatment. The best of them adhere to the ethical principles and practice guidelines of the National Association of Therapeutic Schools and Programs (NATSAP, www.natsap.org).

Boot camp programs, in contrast, tend to be highly confrontational and punitive. The treatment philosophy of such programs is often based on the theory that willful teens need to be broken down, often through degrading confrontation and deprivation of basic needs.[1] This treatment approach is not supported as effective by research.

Indeed, the outcome of this sort of approach is generally a child who complies with expectations while the threat of punishment is held over his head, but then continues to be defiant once he is out of that environment. Indeed, this type of approach actually appears to fuel an adolescent's resentment of adults and authority. Fortunately, very few of these types of programs still exist, though there are vestiges of this outdated treatment philosophy in programs that do not advertise themselves as boot camps.

Recently, there has been concern raised in the media and in Congress about the lack of regulations governing the practices of boot camps, therapeutic wilderness programs, and therapeutic schools. These concerns have valid roots in the experiences of families and teens who were clearly victims of substandard and inadequate care in a few therapeutic programs. As a psychologist practicing in this industry, I am appalled by any practices that threaten the safety and well-being of the families we serve. I do not intend for this book to be a blanket endorsement of every therapeutic program. Instead, I want it to be a resource to help parents make an informed decision about these programs. I have great faith in the therapeutic work that occurs in the many fine therapeutic schools and programs in the country. I believe these schools and programs are meeting a critical need for struggling teens who are not being served adequately by public schools and community-based programs.

served. However, I have preserved the essence of their stories, because I believe these real-life illustrations best capture the principles I describe in this book.

Why I wrote this book

The idea for this book arose out of the conversations I've had with parents like you. Over the years in my work as an adolescent psychologist, I heard numerous stories of how parents get to crisis points with their adolescents, and though each story was unique, the themes were consistently similar. Parents taught me much about how difficult it is to raise children into mature young adults in this day and age, where technology and culture interface in such a way that skills related to delay of gratification and frustration tolerance seldom get used.

As I've listened to parents struggle to put a name to their kids' difficulties, I've been struck by how often they tell me that the therapeutic community has not given them any clear explanation for *why* their kids behave as they do. Yet, descriptive labels are common. Who hasn't heard of a child, perhaps yours, who has been labeled by professionals as having attention deficit-hyperactivity disorder (ADHD), depression, anxiety, oppositional defiant disorder, or bi-polar disorder. One frustrated mother explained how her child's psychologist performed a $3,000-evaluation, and then informed her that her child is oppositional defiant. "Duh!" she exclaimed. "I paid you all this money to tell me what I already knew???"

Many children receive several of these diagnoses at once and are prescribed a combination of psychotropic medications (often called "cocktails"). But most of their parents soon discover the serious limita-

Second Guessing

When parents enroll their child in a therapeutic program, they often feel that their decision is misunderstood by their colleagues and peers. One parent told me recently:

"Other parents think that we are overreacting by sending our son away to a therapeutic school. They think he is a charming and typical adolescent boy, doing what teenagers do. But they do not live with the consequences of his behavior! They don't spend sleepless nights worried about his safety and his ability to make good decisions —they don't lie awake at night trying to digest the awful things he said during the last argument!"

And, indeed, they do not.

tions in this medical approach to diagnosing and treating the problems teens are facing. You see, while we focus our efforts at removing some particular symptom, we often lose sight of the broader context in which teens are exhibiting these symptoms. We forget that teens are in a time of immense change; they are in the process of developing a stable sense of identity; and they are establishing their own particular way of understanding how the world works. Teens are also crystallizing an approach to the demands of daily life that they will use as a template for solving the increasingly complex life challenges they will face in adulthood. So, while medication may alleviate the depressed or anxious mood, a troubled teen's faulty approach to understanding and solving life's challenges may persist and continue to result in poor coping patterns, relationships problems, and failures in school or work. Until the problematic or immature approach is addressed, you will likely see the teen continue to struggle to move forward effectively in his or her life.

My hope in writing this book is that I can provide you with a clear explanation of why teenagers like yours are struggling. It is not rocket science. It is actually age-old wisdom that has become obscured by the medical approach to adolescent difficulties. Once you understand your child's problems within a context of development, you will see clearly what your parental role should be.

I also hope to help you understand how therapeutic schools, residential treatment centers, and wilderness therapy programs address teen problems. I want to educate you a bit about the process you're likely to encounter if you send your child to one of these therapeutic schools or programs. Having walked this path with a large number of families, I have a good understanding of both the practical and the emotional impact on parents. Therapeutic programs are structured in ways that restrict certain privileges, and at times this can be very frustrating and inconvenient for families. I want to help you understand what some of these restrictions might be (though, of course, each program will differ) and provide a rationale for why these are necessary.

I want to speak to what you as a parent are likely to feel while your child is away. Parents of teens in therapeutic programs often need support to manage the emotional burden involved in sending their child away for such a long period. They need to understand that such a decision, especially in circumstances where teens are not being helped by traditional methods and approaches, is a courageous act of good parenting. Most of all, I want you to understand that you are not alone. I hope, in reading this, you will recognize that the feelings and beliefs that you suspected were your solitary burden to bear are actually quite normal.

Finally, I want to offer hope about the possibility of transformation through this experience, for you as well as your child. Psychiatrist Elaine Heffner, in her book *Mothering: The Emotional Experience of Mothering After Freud and Feminism*, writes:

> *The 'universal moments' of child rearing are in fact nothing less than a confron- tation with the most basic problems of living in society: a facing through one's children of all the conflicts inherent in human relationships, a clarification of issues that were unresolved in one's own growing up. The experience of child rearing not only can strengthen one as an individual but also presents the opportu- nity to shape human relationships of the future.*[2]

In this moment of child rearing in which you now find yourself, you are clearly dealing with much more than just being a parent to your child. Indeed, you are being challenged to look yourself and your culture square in the eye, and to ask questions of each. Without a doubt, the way you resolve this crisis with your child will impact you and the com- munity in which your child lives. While this particular moment may be a time of crisis, I want to suggest that it is really an opportunity to reflect, heal and grow. My hope is that this book can aid you in examining both yourself and the cultural assumptions and practices that guide how we act as parents, especially how we respond when our children are in trouble!

I want you to understand that the decision to send a child away so that he or she can become healthier and can create a life worth living necessarily involves changes in the whole family system. If your child is to change, you will need to change, too. Albert Einstein once said: "No problem can be solved by the consciousness that created it." Developing a new consciousness of parenting is absolutely necessary in order to help your child develop into a mature and effective adult.

Over the years, I've observed that children whose parents are willing to "do their own work" fare much better than those who resist taking a good, honest look at themselves. I want to offer some suggestions for what "doing your work" might involve, so that this decision sparks a transformation that you will share with your child.

Let's get started.

---

[1] Merchant, Michael J. "Troubled teens need proven intervention, not boot camp: Seven questions to help parents find a safe and effective alternative." http://www.natsap.org/pa_wildernessrisk.asp (2006).

[2] Heffner, Elaine. *Mothering: The Emotional Experience of Motherhood after Freud and Feminism.* (New York: Doubleday, 1978) preface

CHAPTER ONE

A DIFFICULT CHOICE

Should you send your child away to a therapeutic program?

Despite how difficult things become with their teens, despite the intensity and severity of their problems, when parents are advised to send their child away to a therapeutic school, they often feel bewildered and dismayed. It seems so drastic, so expensive. They are saddened by the prospect of being apart from their child, of not being involved in their adolescent's daily life. These feelings that parents experience are real and valid, and we'll explore them throughout this book. For now, though, let's discuss the practical realities that confront so many parents of struggling teens.

The realities of American culture today make it very difficult to effectively treat many struggling teens while they remain in their home environments. When anguished parents ask me if it is really necessary to send their kid away to a therapeutic school or program, my answer usually involves these considerations:

- The limitations of outpatient treatment options for adolescent difficulties;
- The lack of a cohesive community model for raising children; and
- The challenges and choices facing 21st century adolescents.

The Limitations of Outpatient Treatment

During the years I have worked in residential therapeutic programs, I have never met a teen resident for whom this was the first intervention. Quite the contrary, the parents and teens I meet usually have tried every available option short of long-term residential care, and still have not experienced any significant relief from the distress the teen's problems are creating.

I began my career working in outpatient settings, and I have often wondered if I really helped any of my adolescent patients in any lasting way. Don't get me wrong, I believe it is possible to help some adolescents with an outpatient therapy model, which usually involves an hour per week of individual therapy, perhaps supplemented with family counseling and guidance for parents. Yet, far too many teens seem disengaged from the outpatient therapeutic process. I believe this is the result of shortcomings in the therapeutic approach itself, rather than a problem with the non-responding teen.

Many teens, particularly those with whom I have worked in residential programs, have not yet developed an ability to observe and analyze their experience. This ability to apply insights gained from a weekly therapy session to the rest of one's life is generally a prerequisite to being able to benefit from therapy. And, while some are able to develop this ability while engaging in a therapeutic relationship with a professional, many of the struggling teens I meet are too driven by their impulses to have the necessary self-objectivity that outpatient therapy requires. In other words, the struggling teens I meet are typically those who cannot or will not reflect upon their experience to discern meaningful patterns in their

Mixed Results

Scotty was 14 when his parents began sending him to weekly therapy. They were concerned about how angry Scotty was towards them, and how defiant he was to authority figures in general. Scotty did not want to go to therapy, and saw it as a punishment, even though he had a comfortable rapport with his counselor. During their sessions, the counselor and Scotty would spend a few minutes talking about video games and movies, and then the counselor would gradually probe into situations where Scotty might have felt angry or defiant towards authority figures during the week.

It often took a good bit of probing from the counselor to identify a situation that he and Scotty could explore together. Once they did, the counselor would ask Scotty how he had felt or what he was thinking when the situation occurred. Scotty's responses were typically limited to "I don't know" or "I felt mad." These conversations provided the counselor with an opportunity to empathize with Scotty about how difficult it can be to have to follow rules or expectations that you do not necessarily agree with or understand. He would attempt to help Scotty understand why certain expectations were necessary, and then he and Scotty would role-play the scenarios to help Scotty express his feelings without being so defiant. By the end of the session, Scotty and his counselor were often able to role-play scenarios effectively, and it seemed that Scotty "got it." However, Scotty's real-life anger and defiance continued. His parents and teachers saw little evidence of improvement in how he followed their rules. Scotty continued to believe that he was going to therapy as a punishment, and while he liked talking with his counselor each week, he did not seem to internalize the fact that he needed to make real changes in his approach to dealing with authority.

behavior or maladaptive ways in which they cope with experiences and relationships. And because their coping patterns are so inappropriate, there is often an urgency on the part of parents and professionals to use the quickest, easiest method to ease the teen's distress and inhibit behaviors that may be dangerous or that are causing failures across the various dimensions of their lives.

No Panacea in the Medicine Cabinet

In many families, medical interventions are relied upon to help struggling teens and their parents. If a child is having trouble concentrating in school, there is a medication for that. If a child is moody or irritable, there is a medication for that, too. To be frank, commercials shown during prime-time television may lead you to believe that there is a medication for every problem known to humans. Unfortunately, I believe we are far too quick to place struggling teens on medications. I say this because I have seen so many teens arrive at a wilderness program or a residential therapeutic school on a regimen of medications that has not necessarily helped them function better in their home and school environments (otherwise they would not be in a therapeutic program). Often, once they are settled in a structured therapeutic environment, medication can gradually be tapered down or even discontinued. And, according to the teens, their parents, and my observations, they are able to actually function at a higher level than they did while on the medication regimen. But, of course, the reality is that pharmaceutical treatments tend to be more cost-effective than other interventions, and certainly do not require the kinds of environmental changes that may be necessary to help the teen function better in society.

This love affair with the "quick fix" is a manifestation of our American *Zeitgeist*, or spirit of our times. We desperately seek to remove symptoms of distress with the least amount of cost and the fewest changes to our way of life. And, to be sure, millions of people benefit from medical treatments for mental illness and psychological discomfort. But, is this approach helping children and adolescents develop a more mature approach to life? Once they are medicated, are they more capable of dealing effectively with life's challenges? I believe some do benefit from a medical intervention when it enables them to learn from their environment so that they become more mature in their thinking and problem solving. For a large number of teens, however, much needed environmental changes do not accompany the medication routine. And, while their distress may be somewhat reduced by medication, they continue to approach the world in a problematic and immature way.

Over the last 25 years, the focus of mental health treatment has become fixated on symptom reduction, and many clinicians now give little consideration to the context in which symptoms occur. If young Jimmy demonstrates difficulty sustaining his concentration in school, we no longer ask questions about his developmental history, his family life, the amount of quality time he spends with adults in focused activities, or the number of hours he plays video games with a stimulation level equivalent to a day at war. We do not consider his learning style, the way in which a curriculum is being taught, or the number of equally rowdy students in his classroom. No, we diagnose him with ADHD, prescribe him Ritalin or Adderall, and consider the job done! Certainly, many professionals in the child and adolescent mental health field do consider these developmental and environmental variables, but our solutions are addressing these things less and less.

Symptom reduction became the primary goal of adolescent treatment when managed-care companies began pushing clinicians to demonstrate measurable results in the least amount of time possible. If research indicated that a certain outcome could be achieved, practitioners were expected to make it happen. Not surprisingly, the field has gradually shifted its focus to technology to reduce unwanted symptoms. Today, fewer and fewer practitioners focus on healthy self-development in our children and adolescents, or on how to parent in such a way that we help young people acquire mature ways of dealing with life and relationships.

The sad reality, the tragic reality, is that managed care is forcing practitioners into this symptom-focused approach through its decisions about which treatments it will reimburse and which it will not. The result is that more and more clinicians are altering their practice to qualify for insurance payments; institutions are training their staffs to ensure reimbursement; and consumers are being sold on the premise that "medical intervention is the way to go!" Too few of us are questioning this approach—until it is our child who does not want to go to school or leave his room and his video games.

What we have lost in the medical approach to treating behavioral and mood disturbances are plausible theories that explain why these disturbances occur. Many of us have come to assume that a depressed mood is caused by a chemical imbalance in the brain, and that a pill that restores that balance is the answer. Even psychologists and social workers, who tend to be the providers of talk therapy and other non-medical interventions, have been drawn into tailoring their work for the sole purpose of symptom reduction. Psychological research, for example, defines a successful intervention as one that produces a statistically significant reduction in symptomatic behavior in a randomized sample of people complaining of the symptom. But it often stops short of explaining why the symptom is occurring in the first place.

Why Counseling Often Fails

Most of the adolescents and families with whom I work are all too familiar with the weekly routine of sitting in a room with a therapist and talking about the sordid details of their lives: how they feel about their mom and dad, how they interact with their families, what draws them to their friends, what they want to be when they grow up. Outpatient therapists are doing their best to provide care within this medical paradigm, but let's face it: Adolescents are good at snowing their therapists. One hour per week sessions can create a comfortable rapport between the therapist and his teen patient, but it is not enough to create the kind of relationship and involvement that will produce the maturity that we are hoping for.

Likewise, I believe that adolescents are often too influenced by their social environment and peers to really benefit from one-on-one therapy. For some, even when individual therapy is paired with family therapy, it is still not enough to mitigate the impact of the peer group, what Ron Taffel calls "the second family."[1] Teenagers may mean what they say to a therapist, but to apply their insight and intentions to their social and academic worlds may be much more than they are yet capable of doing.

For problem adolescents, there are always at least two levels at which their problems need to be addressed. There is the behavioral and symptomatic level, which is what generally leads families to doctors and therapists in the first place (e.g., irritability towards parents, defiance of authority, etc.). And then there is the developmental level. During adolescence, a teen's physiology is changing at the highest rate since infancy; their brains are exploding with cell production. At the same time, their psychosocial development is reaching a point where they are trying new approaches to their lives and their relationships. Understanding how these two levels interact is extremely important in considering how best to intervene with struggling teens.

For a large number of troubled teens, their real problem is immaturity. I came to this conclusion while working alongside Dr. John McKinnon and Dr. John Santa, founders of one of the finest therapeutic boarding schools in the country, Montana Academy. Teens go to outpatient therapists and psychiatrists because they are feeling depressed or anxious, because they are exhibiting problematic behavior, or because they are unable to focus in the classroom. However, as McKinnon and Santa helped me understand, the reasons these and other distressing symptoms tend to persist despite outpatient therapy or medical intervention is that struggling teens often approach their world in an immature and ineffective way.

By approach, I am referring to the guiding assumptions and expectations that allow an individual to organize experiences, make sense of them, and act upon them. All of us have a unique approach to life and relationships, whether we are consciously aware of our guiding assumptions or not. For example, while a toddler may approach the problem of being hungry by throwing a temper tantrum until mom makes a sandwich, an adolescent is expected to approach the problem of hunger in a very different way. Often, however, when you look at the issues struggling teens are facing and the way they are approaching them, you can clearly see that their assumptions about problems and their methods of resolving them are similar to those used by younger children. As their lives and problems become more complex throughout adolescence, an immature approach can create numerous failures, which may result in significant behavioral and emotional disturbances.

Helping children grow up and develop a mature approach to their lives and relationships requires an appropriate balance of *attunement* (attentiveness, nurturance) to their physical and psychological needs and *containment* (supervision, limit-setting, discipline) within the context of *significant relationships* and *attachments.* Symptom-focused approaches assume that kids already have these factors at work in their lives, and that the reduction of symptoms should be enough to put them back on track for normal healthy development. And that is quite true for some, if not most, adolescents who are experiencing trouble, but it is certainly not the case for all of them.

The Missing Model for Parents

One of the most important developmental tasks for adolescents to accomplish is learning how to adhere to and respect societal standards and rules. Yet, parents who set appropriate limits for their children are often thwarted by other parents. I believe this is largely because we as a society do not understand very well what adolescents can and cannot handle effectively. We lack a cohesive community model for setting limits with our teenagers, and parents tend to be so anxious about being stricter than other parents, that they may adopt a kind of "keeping up with the Jones's" mentality.

If it takes a village to raise a child, we must expect that a village raising kids into healthy adults will have some consensus about what is appropriate and what is not. I am certainly not suggesting some moral throwback to a past culture of repression and restriction. Rather, I am suggesting that we have forgotten how appropriate limits contribute to the process of growing up. Indulgent parenting, I believe, is not about what is best for the child, but what is easiest or most conflict-free for the parent.

As we talk about the ways teens suffer because of their immaturity, I hope it will become apparent to you that the lack of reasonable consistency in limit-setting among parents in our villages actually prevents our teens from growing up and enjoying balanced lives. It is also one of the primary reasons why sending struggling kids away to therapeutic schools and programs is at times necessary in order to help them flourish.

Confronting Social and Cultural Challenges

As children move into adolescence, they become subject to a new set of expectations and demands. Schoolwork becomes more rigorous and time-consuming. Teens not only have to stay alert in class to learn the material, they also must organize their time and use self-discipline in order to get the heavier load of homework done. If they are involved in extra-curricular activities, they must factor them into their schedule and learn how to prioritize what they do and when they do it. As the looming college application process gets closer, they must begin researching schools and universities, obtain application materials, prepare to take college entrance exams, and build relationships with teachers who would be willing to write recommendations about their academic performance and character.

Poor Neighboring

Families I speak with frequently report that they are not supported in their efforts to parent by other parents. This is especially true in regard to limit-setting. The teens confirm this, telling me about friend's "cool" parents, who actually allow their kids to smoke marijuana or drink alcohol at their homes. "We'd rather they do it here where they are safe!" is how indulgent parents defend their actions.

This type of parenting is not only an example of foolish parenting, it is an example of poor neighboring to the community of parents attempting to maintain appropriate limits for their teens. Let's face it, overly indulgent parents not only undermine the limit-setting of other parents, whose kids will quickly raise a ruckus about how John's parents let him do this or that, they also model for teens a disdain for strict limits and authority. At times, they even facilitate teens in disregarding parents' rules.

Their social environment also becomes much more complex. Teens compare themselves to their peer group and try to create a consistent identity across a wide range of groups. This, as anyone who recalls their teen years knows, is one of the greatest challenges of growing up. Dealing with pressures to conform, choosing who to identify with and who not to, and learning to take risks responsibly, all while being true to one's emerging idea of oneself are not tasks for the weary or the immature. Further complicating matters are the often brutal waves of gossip or social humiliation that teens dish out against each other.

At this age, drug and alcohol use become prevalent, and every teen must decide how to manage that temptation, while enduring the inevitable reputation issues that arise from aligning themselves with those who *don't* or those who *do*. Furthermore, teens are learning to manage their emerging sexuality at a time in their lives when every romantic encounter is a potential landmine for self-esteem. Making it all the more difficult is the fact that they are coming of age in a world that no longer values dignity and respect, where sexual encounters are captured on cell phones and made public, and where 11- and 12-year-olds speak openly and knowingly about hand-jobs or going down on someone.

And then there are family relationships. Navigating the changing relationships with mom and dad, moving away from childish dependence and defining oneself as separate and unique from one's parents, creates confusing and emotionally loaded tension. One of the best book titles that captures this tension is *Get Out of My Life, but First Could You Drive Me and Cheryl to the Mall?* by Anthony E. Wolf. Teens want so badly to be independent, but they are not. Often they act like they are, copping an attitude and flaunting their expensive possessions, even when their parents' money paid for them. Ideally, as teens move through adolescence and are given more opportunities to manage their independence, they are able to act responsibly and safely, demonstrating their emerging maturity.

All of these life changes take place on a playing field that is saturated with distractions. The wireless generation is always plugged in to something. They text message while driving a car or eating dinner. They keep a dozen conversations going through instant messaging, while downloading songs or viewing video clips. They search through MySpace for friends or intriguing people, and spice up their own profile to make it more interesting. While doing their homework, they also play games on PlayStation. Teen life today begins to mimic the information superhighway, where everything is at your fingertips and the next stimulus is only .3 seconds away!

REAL TIME

A Different World

Today's teens, perhaps more than at any previous period in history, are in over their heads. The choices facing adolescents today are much more complex than many of them are capable of managing, especially given the lack of parental supervision that's common in American families.

Through the Internet, everything is available to teens, from pornography to bomb making directions to sites for buying drugs. And, as many of you know, teens are much more savvy than adults at getting to the sites they want. One family I worked with discovered that their adolescent son had gambled away thousands of dollars (using dad's credit card) through a site that appears to be selling phone cards!

And although many of the sites that teens browse are benign, I believe too many teens are being given free reign to a world that requires a level of maturity they do not have. One needs only look at the MySpace pages of many teens to confirm this.

Unfortunately, many teens are not able to manage the new game of adolescence very effectively. As teens are confronted with all the demands from the academic, social, familial, and self-identity realms of their life, they must use a different set of guiding assumptions and values than those that got them through childhood. Many *do* develop a mature approach, but many *don't*. In many ways, adolescence becomes the great divide between those who are "getting it," and acting in a more mature way, and those who are clinging relentlessly to the outdated approaches of childhood.

Ron Taffel is a psychologist practicing in New York and the author of several books about adolescent therapy. Taffel emphasizes that today's teens live in a very different world than their parents did, primarily due to the technological intrusion of the internet, cell phones, iPods, and 500 channels of television. The impact, according to Taffel, is that many of today's teens have internalized a chaotic, stimulus-driven relationship to their world. In a commentary published in *Psychotherapy Networker*, "The Divided Self: Inside the World of 21st-Century Teens," he writes:

> *Decades ago, most kids carried parents around inside, whether they wanted to or not. Through endless channels, parents constituted a deeply felt, internal presence, however neurotic and oppressive it might sometimes have been. But what I encounter again and again in my practice is the startling reality that many parents have become psychically extruded from the inner lives of their children.*[2]

Many of the teens that I see are easily distracted and do not tolerate frustration very well. They also do not tolerate the slower pace of real time, where bursts of excitement are interspersed with lulls of silence and inactivity. One of the main complaints I hear from teens is that they hate feeling bored. Much of their acting out, including drug use and risk-taking behavior, they attribute to boredom. They enjoy virtual reality, filled with endless information and stimulation, but find riding in the car with mom or dad painful without their iPod.

Because teens are so plugged in and have so many distractions available, it is difficult to pull the plug and help them develop critical skills, such as frustration tolerance, healthy self-soothing, and real-life socializing with another human being. Their ability to develop a clear sense of themselves also is impacted by the numerous distractions they face. In many of the teens I counsel, I sense a vacancy. Perhaps this is why, when asked how they feel about something, a remarkable number of them respond with "I don't know."

The Rise of Therapeutic Programs

Because of the concerns listed above, the number of therapeutic schools and programs has soared during the past two decades. Whereas in the 1980s, there were only a handful of these programs, today there are hundreds of schools that advertise themselves as emotional growth schools, therapeutic boarding schools, or residential treatment centers. In addition, there are a number of outdoor behavioral health programs that take place in wilderness settings.

Therapeutic schools and programs fill the gap in mental health care that occurred when long-term hospitalization programs became a thing of the past. They also provide families with an alternative to boot camp programs and military schools. However, the bulk of these programs were established in response to the serious shortcomings of outpatient treatment in meeting the needs of many struggling teens and their families.

Though many people still believe that troubled teenagers are best served when they remain in their home environment, too many young people are falling through the cracks of mainstream care. For these teens, therapeutic schools and programs provide an alternative to traditional outpatient counseling by combining a variety of programming options and therapeutic approaches to help young people develop maturity and direction. For example, some schools are on ranches where the teens work with horses, sheep, and other farm animals. Some are in urban areas where students participate in community service and attend local cultural events. One program even offers group training for a triathlon as one of its guiding structures.

Regardless of the particular emphasis or climate of these programs, each provides a cohesive, structured community for teens. They are places where teens are expected to live up to clear standards and where mature behavior is modeled and taught by responsible adults. Most of these treatment facilities function as "villages," where teens can gain the experiences they need to develop character and maturity away from many of the distractions that they are not yet able to manage effectively. Many programs provide individualized academic plans that are tailored to help teens learn how to learn. The best programs also empower parents and provide support for carrying out the important work of helping their children grow up.

So, how well does it work? According to a growing body of literature, outcomes for teens who complete therapeutic schools and programs look very promising. A 2006 study by Dr. Ellen Behrens and Kristen Satterfield of Canyon Research Consulting, Inc., Salt Lake City, Utah, sampled nearly 1,000 students enrolled in private residential treatment programs and found significant improvements in family relationships, communication with parents, and compliance with expectations and rules.[3] They also observed a significant reduction in problems from admission to discharge on each measure of psycho-social functioning and nearly every clinical syndrome measured.

Similar findings were reported by Dr. Keith C. Russell, a professor at the University of Minnesota. He documented reductions in "presenting symptoms" for youths enrolled in outdoor behavioral health programs at discharge, and at three and six months post-treatment.[4] In another study, Russell measured outcomes at 24 months post-treatment, and discovered that the majority of teens were doing well in school and in family communication, as determined by self-reporting measures completed by teens and their parents.[5]

And Dr. Nick Hong of Montana Academy reported preliminary findings that teens show improvement on measures of maturity while in a therapeutic boarding school environment.[6] In my own experience, parents of teens that I have worked with in these therapeutic programs regularly call to tell me that their kids are making it in the world, standing on their own two feet, and demonstrating maturity in their approach to their lives. Most of my colleagues report similar experiences. That is why I believe therapeutic schools and programs can be an exciting and life-changing option for struggling adolescents and their families.

[1] Taffel, Ron. *Breaking Through to Teens: A New Psychotherapy for the New Adolescence.* (New York: Guilford, 2005).

[2] Taffel, Ron. "The divided self: Inside the world of 21st-century teens." *Psychotherapy Networker* (July/Aug. 2006). www.psychotherapynetworker.org.

[3] Behrens, E. and K. Satterfield. "Report of findings from a multi-center study of youth outcomes in private residential treatment." Paper presented at the 114th Annual Convention of the American Psychological Association at New Orleans, Louisiana. (August 2006).

[4] Russell, K.C. "A longitudinal assessment of treatment outcomes in outdoor behavioral healthcare." Technical Report 28. (Idaho Falls Forest Wildlife and Range Experiment Station. Moscow, ID: 2002).

[5] Russell, K.C. "Two Years Later: A qualitative assessment of youth well-being and the role of aftercare in outdoor behavioral healthcare treatment." *Child and Youth Care Forum* 34, no. 3, (2005): 209-239.

[6] Hong, N. "Family functioning in adolescents in therapeutic schools and programs." Paper presented at the conference of the National Association of Therapeutic Schools and Programs at La Jolla, California. (January 2007).

CHAPTER TWO

THE INTERSECTION OF ADOLESCENCE

When does immaturity require intervention?

A friend of mine, who is the mother of a 16-year-old, likes to joke that she is trying to raise an adult, not a child! The humor and irony here, of course, is that our popular expression, "raising a child," has always implicitly meant that we are raising them to be responsible adults. Yet, our parenting culture, indeed the culture at large, quite often appears to be turning out adults who act like children!

Nowhere is this more apparent than among teens who are struggling to meet the demands of adolescent life. Their struggles take many forms, from school failure to substance abuse to defiance of parents and authority to self-destructive behaviors. For a large number of struggling teens, these problems signify a problem in development, what McKinnon and Santa call "developmental delay syndrome."* The defining characteristic of developmental delay syndrome is a persistently immature approach to life and relationships. A teen's persistent immaturity can lead to a number of failures, especially as they face the increasingly complex demands and expectations of late adolescence. If this immature approach is not adequately addressed during adolescence, it may lead to a personality disorder in adulthood. Personality disorders tend to be rigidly maladap-

---

*Throughout this chapter, I will be expanding on the developmental delay formulation that I learned while working with Dr. John McKinnon and Dr. John Santa of Montana Academy.

tive patterns of relating to others and of regulating internal experiences. As such, they are often quite debilitating and resistant to treatment.

In this chapter, let's look at the kinds of problems that lead teens into residential treatment. You'll see that many of these are symptoms of an immature approach to relationships, self-regulation, and goal-oriented behavior. Fortunately, there are effective intervention methods for dealing with these problems, and we'll explore how therapeutic schools and programs provide appropriate intervention for struggling teens and their families.

Making Sense of Adolescent Problems

Adolescents entering therapeutic programs generally share common problems or symptoms. Here are a few voiced by parents when enrolling their child into a therapeutic program:

- Defiant behavior towards parents (not following rules, ignoring curfew, etc.)
- Irritable and unpredictable moods
- Problems in school
- Lack of effort in schoolwork; poor or failing grades
- Poor choice of friends
- Verbal abuse towards family members
- Extremely self-centered, with strong feelings of entitlement
- Emotional outbursts
- Withdrawal into computer games or Internet
- Lying
- Stealing from family members or stores
- Low self-esteem
- Self-harm (e.g., cutting or burning self)
- Impulsivity (acting without concern for consequences)
- Refusal to help around the house, complete chores, etc.
- Drug and alcohol abuse

As we look at the problems listed, we can certainly see indications of diagnosable disorders. For example, impulsivity and problems in school are quite common among those diagnosed with attention deficit-hyperactivity disorder (ADHD). Irritable and unpredictable moods, lack of effort in schoolwork, and low self-esteem are common symptoms of a mood disorder, either depression or anxiety. Defiant behavior and verbal abuse towards family members is often associated with oppositional defiant disorder, while lying and stealing are symptoms often associated with conduct disorder. And while a large majority of teens arrive at therapeutic programs having already been diagnosed with one or several of these disorders, I believe we must view these symptoms within the context of the tremendous developmental changes that occur during adolescence.

Adolescence is one of the most intense and significant periods in a child's development. It is the crossroad where a new "way of being" begins. Childish approaches to dealing with the challenges of life become ineffective, and if held onto too long, even pathological. A teen's dependency on others (usually parents) to solve problems and meet all his or her needs begins to wane. By late adolescence, teenagers are expected to become increasingly independent as they prepare to be launched into the world of adult responsibilities.

During these years, the rules for relationships evolve. Teens are shedding the self-absorption and feelings of entitlement that characterized childhood relationships and beginning to exhibit greater mutuality and reciprocity in relationships. Approaches to problem-solving also change, partly due to the increasing complexity of the problems teens face, and partly due to the enormity of the consequences—addiction, unwanted pregnancy, arrests—that await those whose decision-making skills are poor or unrealistic. And, finally, well-adjusted teens are acquiring healthy and effective ways of regulating their emotions and impulses in order to be successful in their endeavors.

Adolescence is the in-between time, the intersection of childhood and adulthood. In fact, as developmental psychologist Dr. Robert Kegan explains, the very word *adolescence* comes from the Latin verb, *adolescere,* which literally means "to grow up."

The past participle of the same word is adultus, 'having grown up,' or 'grown-up.' The word adolescence, then, suggests that by looking at what a culture asks its youth to 'grow up to,' we can discover that culture's definition of adulthood. [1]

I often ask the parents of teens I counsel what kind of adult they want their teenager to become. Typically, after a few moments' reflection, their responses are remarkably similar. Time and time again I hear that they want their children to become adults who are dependable, trustworthy, and caring; who think before they act; who are good citizens; and who know how to find happiness in their lives and relationships. Parents generally aren't so concerned about what career their kids choose or where they go to school, but they do care about what kind of student, employee, or neighbor they will be.

If children are to become the kind of adults that we've described above, then it is critical that they begin to demonstrate these qualities during their adolescence. By middle to late adolescence, teens who are developing a mature and stable character should be approaching the various dimensions of their world more like adults and less like children.[2] The good news is that most teens are capable of developing such a character. The not so good news is that their environments do not always provide the kinds of experiences that are necessary for this development to occur.

In chapter one, I explained that one of the primary reasons that teens are not being adequately treated in their home communities is that there are serious limitations to the medical model in solving adolescent problems. The writings of Daniel Siegel (*The Developing Mind*), Madeline Levine (*The Price of Privilege*), David Walsh (*Why Do They Act That Way?*), Robert Kegan (*The Evolving Self*), and Robert Brooks & Sam Goldstein (*Raising a Self-Disciplined Child*) provide contemporary support for the notion that an adolescents' developmental environment must be considered carefully before explaining or intervening in their behavioral and emotional symptoms.

There is no pill or 15-session counseling intervention that I am aware of that will make immature teens grow up and approach their decisions with more maturity. And, because our culture is so full of distractions for children, teens, and their parents, the necessary work of parenting and pushing immature teens to grow up is often very difficult. Add to this the availability of drugs and the incredible power of immature peer groups, and you can see why struggling teens often are referred to residential programs to accomplish the tasks required to grow up.

Let's continue our discussion of teens' developmental struggles by looking at their problems with immaturity in relationships, self-regulation, and goal-oriented behavior.

Problems in Relationships

In the initial interview with parents of struggling teens, I often ask them to describe their relationship with their teen. Here are some of their responses.

In the past, our relationship was loving and friendly. During the past year-and-a- half, the relationship has declined. Currently, our son's behavior is hostile, defensive, hurtful, mocking. He uses profanity towards us, avoids us, refuses to eat with us or help with chores. He is beginning to resort to violence.

Our daughter is very close to us. However, she has become very manipulative and lies often to us. She is constantly badgering us for something, and, quite frankly, wears us down. She often promises to do something but doesn't follow through.

Our son is frequently angry and verbally abusive to us if we try to hold him accountable. He is extremely irritable and unpredictable, and we feel like we are walking on eggshells in our home.

She strongly resists the parental authority of both parents. She is more argumentative with her mom and tries to triangulate mom versus dad. She can be a bully towards mom, making threats and trying to make her feel guilty for not allowing her to do certain things.

He won't listen to us. He treats the whole family like we are second-class citizens. He refuses our limits, rolls his eyes at us, and sometimes leaves without telling us where he is going. Last time, he didn't return for two days.

Children approach relationships differently than most adults. For children, relationships tend to be one-sided—"you exist to satisfy me"—whereas in healthy adult relationships there is a balance of give-and-take. Similarly, children-adult relationships are necessarily characterized by the child's dependency on the adult: "I can't drive myself to soccer practice, so I must depend on you." In adult relationships, however, individuals take responsibility for meeting their own needs. While adults may look to others to meet certain needs, they do so with the understanding that those adults have no real obligation to do so.

When we look at the critical developmental process that occurs between the ages of 12 to 18, we can see that it is important that adolescents relinquish a childish, self-centered, dependent approach to relationships, and assume an approach that will allow them to form lasting, adult relationships. The obstacle for teens with developmental delay syndrome, according to McKinnon and Santa, is that they tend to be narcissistic and to lack empathy for others.

Childish Narcissism

There is a time in life when narcissism is appropriate and expected. Very young children require that their needs are a top priority of their caregivers. They believe the world revolves around them, and, for the very young, it should. However, as young children grow, they encounter inevitable disappointments when their needs are not met. If their critical needs are met reasonably well most of the time, then the inevitable disappointments serve a very important function of frustrating the child's expectation that the universe will revolve around them. In just the right amount, these experiences become what Heinz Kohut termed *optimal frustrations.*[3] The fruit of optimal frustration is that children become aware that their caregivers have priorities that do not involve them. Children, therefore, begin to develop frustration tolerance and self-soothing abilities. Over time, they become more creative problem-solvers, seeking ways to meet their needs themselves.

By the time they reach adolescence, kids should have experienced enough optimal frustrations in their significant relationships to learn that their needs and wants are not the only needs and wants within those relationships. Experiences of optimal frustration do not produce shame in the child for having needs, nor do they result in a serious break in the relationship. Rather, in situations that are optimally frustrating, parents recognize the validity of the child's needs and demonstrate empathy toward the child, recognizing that it is difficult not to have someone always meet your needs. The child is supported in managing her actions when a need is not met, or perhaps not met *now.*

For example, if the child is invited to a friend's house, but mom has another commitment so that she can't drive her there, the child should be able to tolerate the frustration and either find another way to her friend's house or not go. Mom may soothe the child—"Honey, I know you really want to go, but I just can't take you tonight. I know that must be difficult to hear."— but, in the end, she allows her daughter to experience the disappointment, to experience it *fully* under her care. In this way, her daughter has an opportunity to practice soothing herself and dealing with disappointment, which will prepare her for many more such experiences in her life.

It is a beautiful thing when an adolescent finally understands that mom and dad are not put here on earth to satisfy his every demand. Usually this process takes years to complete. However, once the groundwork is laid, the teen's ability to develop mutual relationships emerges. This sets the stage for the tasks of intimacy development that await him. However, if a teen fails to "get it," and thinks that mom or dad exist for the sole purpose of catering to him, it can create a truly ugly situation. The teen's demanding behavior, his fury when he does not get what he wants, and his overall lack of gratitude would make any parent nauseous.

Many of the parents I speak with know this scenario well. When their child wants something or needs to be somewhere, the parents are not supposed to have conflicting needs or wants. Instead, they are to drop everything and respond to the child. Teens with narcissistic tendencies believe they are entitled to get what they want when they want it, without being required to do anything in return. These feelings of entitlement give rise to the expression "spoiled brat" and, at the same time, appear to fuel the internal emptiness so many privileged teens feel. In fact, clinical psychologist Dr. Madeline Levine points out in *The Price of Privilege* that one of the nation's most at-risk groups for emotional difficulties are preteens and teens from affluent, well-educated families.[4] Levine suggests that these teens often lack appreciation for all the advantages they have, possibly because they have not learned how to tolerate frustration. In other words, many of these kids have not endured enough optimal frustrations to spark a more mature understanding of relationships.

Many of you will recognize this narcissistic approach in your adolescents. Some of you, however, may read this and think: "My child is not narcissistic. If anything, she has very low self-esteem. She feels she can't be successful at anything and is very depressed." Let me remind you, I am not necessarily describing arrogant kids. What I am describing is a mindset in which teens view other people as being responsible for meeting their needs and wants, and it's this attitude of entitlement that keeps kids from assuming responsibility for getting what they want.

You can see how narcissism causes problems for teens as they get closer to adulthood. The expectation that their needs should take precedence in close relationships can be a recipe for failure in adult relationships. Such an approach offers no opportunity for true intimacy. After all, to a narcissistic teen or adult, relationships with other people are only good when they satisfy the needs of the narcissistic individual.

Perhaps you are thinking that self-absorption and feelings of entitlement are hallmarks of adolescence—*they're all that way!* That's true to some extent, but as McKinnon points out, immature teens can't seem to get beyond their narcissistic and entitled approach even when situations warrant it. What separates immature teens from their more mature counterparts is that those who are more mature can shift their approach when it is necessary. They can actually let go of their self-absorption and accept and respect the needs of others in a relationship.

Lack of empathy

The parents of immature teens describe to me over and over how their kids just do not seem to get how their behavior affects their family. One girl, Alyssa, sold a precious family ring that belonged to her mother to get money to buy marijuana. When her mother tearfully confronted her, explaining how much this ring meant to her, Alyssa responded: "My God, it's just a ring! I'm sorry it's such a big deal to you!"

An even more extreme example of this lack of empathy was demonstrated by Tim, a 15-year-old boy who arrived at a wilderness program after the "final straw," in which he sent a text message to a peer who had just made a suicide attempt. "I hope you're dead," the message read. Fortunately, in an act of smart parenting, the recipient's father contacted Tim's parents and threatened to charge him with harassment if they did not take action. When I spoke to Tim about this, he said in a tone of annoyance and without remorse: "I didn't mean it."

Adolescents who reach adulthood lacking the ability to incorporate empathy into their relationships and responsibilities are at serious risk of sociopathic and criminal behavior. Perhaps they will end up in the judicial system, perhaps they will not. But, their relationships will undoubtedly be plagued by a lack of respect, and their insensitivity will lead them to hurt those closest to them.

The "Plugged In"

Immature teens are also plagued by other problems in relationships. One that I see more and more frequently is that kids are so consumed with being plugged into some form of technology that they become isolated and alienated from real-world relationships. Internet games have become an obsession for many teens who are already immature and insecure in their relationships. Because of the social component of these virtual games, teens often don't realize that they are, in fact, becoming

Letter from Home

I remember a particular group therapy session that I had with 10 adolescent boys at a wilderness program. One boy read aloud letters from his parents in which they described how his choices and behavior impacted them. He read of his mother's pain from the times he called her terrible names. He read about how his parents would anxiously stay up all night when he would run away, wondering if he was okay, wishing he could consider their feelings and call them to let them know where he was. He read about how his refusal to go to his mother's favorite restaurant on Mother's Day, and the conflict that ensued, not only upset his mom, but hurt her deeply.

There were similar comments in his father's letter, all pointing to this boy's incredible lack of empathy or concern for anyone but himself. When he was finished reading, I asked him what it was like to read those comments. He paused for a moment, and said: "I didn't know I was so bad to my family."

I found his obliviousness to the impact he was having on his family hard to believe, so I asked the other boys in the group if they could relate. One by one, every other boy in that group confessed that they, too, had never realized that their actions or comments were having such a negative impact on their family.

One particularly articulate boy in the group summed it up: "I always thought that my parents were just supposed to put up with me being angry or unwilling to do what they wanted. They were the parents, I was the child, and that's how I thought it was supposed to be. I never thought about the fact that they have feelings, too. Now I get it that they're not just supposed to be invulnerable to my actions."

alienated. Yet, they interact with others in a cloud of anonymity that prevents anyone from really knowing who they are.

Similarly, I'm concerned that the level of TV-watching, gaming, computer usage, and other distractions that are so prevalent in teens' homes may actually prevent them from having enough *real time* connections with their parents. Psychosocial development requires significant relationships.

Yet, relationships are hard to nurture when teens are isolated by their iPods or immersed in their virtual worlds. And teens who are already somewhat less mature in their relationships are the ones who really need to be engaged with their families without so many distractions. However, as parents can attest, unplugging teens from their electronics can be akin to opening Pandora's box. Temper tantrums, threats, sneakiness, and manipulation are often the burdens parents bear once they pull the plug.

The "Drugged In"

Drugs, alcohol, and the culture surrounding them also can be a tremendous obstacle for struggling teens. There are many concerns that arise when immature adolescents develop an interest in or liking for substances. For many of the families I've met, it's their teen's drug use that facilitates deception and selfishness in their relationships with others. Substance use can prevent teens from developing mature judgment, and it often shields them from the emotional impact of relationships, which immature teens must feel if they hope to achieve a grown-up approach to life. For immature teens, substance use may actually replace primary relationships, and teens will take extreme measures to protect that relationship. Teens will lie, steal, manipulate, and place themselves in risky situations to ensure that they have access to their drug of choice.

Peer relationships between substance-abusing teens typically center around getting and using the drug together. Sadly, these peer groups often consist of other troubled teens. Often they are kids who are going nowhere, who thrive on immediate gratification, but lack the ability to put forth sustained effort towards some meaningful goal. Generally, these teens only value relationships with people who support or enable their addiction and reject those that threaten their commitment to drug use.

Problems with Self-Regulation

Immature teens tend to be described as impulsive, as acting without thought for the consequences of their behavior. The ability to regulate and manage impulses effectively is an important milestone of childhood development. Yet, by the time they reach adolescence, many immature teens still have not developed that capacity. A large number were pre-scribed some form of medication during elementary school to help them control their impulsivity, but most continue to have difficulties regulating their behavior.

These highly impulsive teens often act as if they are immune to the real consequences of their behavior. That is not because they have not experienced consequences, but rather because the consequences they had were inconsistent, or else they were rescued from the most severe consequences by their parents. No wonder these teens believe that the natural consequences of their poor decision-making are worth the gamble. At best, they figure, they won't get caught; at worst, if they are caught, someone will likely bail them out.

All too often, the histories of these immature struggling teens are replete with one rescue after another. Parents, of course, usually try to prop up these struggling adolescents, protect their self-esteem, and so on. But, what is sorely missing for so many of our teens is the experience of cleaning up the mess they've made, even if it is a big mess with signifi-cant ramifications. Rather than partnering with their teens to make amends, many parents assume the responsibility for the clean-up. The result, as I'm sure many of you are aware, is that their children fail to develop a sense of accountability, and they have a weakened capacity for considering the consequences of engaging in a particular behavior.

The medical model has made the problem worse in many instances. By attributing poor decisions to biological causes, there is always an excuse for bad behavior and an argument for reducing the consequences that naturally follow. I certainly agree that there is such a phenomenon as executive functioning disorder, which leads to problems with planning, goal-oriented behavior, and inhibition of impulses. I also do not under-estimate the impact of disorders such as attention deficit-hyperactivity disorder. But I have seen a large number of adolescents, diagnosed as impulsive or deficient in executive functioning, who have rarely had to face the natural consequences of their behavior, a crucial step in devel-oping impulse control abilities.

So is it nature or nurture that is really driving the bad behavior? What researchers of the brain appear to be demonstrating is that the nature vs. nurture dichotomy has been blown way out of proportion. In so many dimensions of psychological development, experience (nurture) actually affects brain structure (nature) and the wiring of neural pathways in the brain.[5]

Facing the natural consequences of decisions and behavior is something that parents can and should do *with* their children, not *for* their children. Instead of rescuing their kids, and shielding them from the impact of natu-ral consequences, parents who are supportively attuned to their children

Bailed Out

Jeremy arrived in the wilderness after his second arrest. His parents had bailed him out of jail on the very day that he had been placed on parole by a judge for a previous charge of shoplifting. That afternoon, while in a CVS pharmacy, Jeremy decided to grab a few candy bars and a soft drink and place them in his coat pocket. He and his friends had done it many times before and had always gotten away with it. However, when Jeremy walked out the CVS door this time, an alarm sounded. He ran, but the store manager chased him down while an employee called the police.

Jeremy's parents negotiated this latest charge by agreeing to send him to a wilderness program, where it quickly became ap- parent that Jeremy thought he was immune to natural consequences. He really did not believe that rules applied to him. Although his parents were obviously frustrated and exhausted from bailing him out of trouble, they always did.

When I asked them about Jeremy's prob- lems, they suggested that he had low self- esteem. Although they would yell at Jeremy about his actions, he knew that when push came to shove, they would rescue him from serious consequences. In fact, he knew the drill so well that he would play up his depres- sion and impulsivity whenever he was chal- lenged on his poor decision-making. This ma- nipulative tactic always triggered his parents to rescue him.

allow natural consequences to occur, recognizing that these are opportuni- ties for learning and problem-solving. Levine sums it up quite nicely:

> *By allowing them to get occasionally bruised in childhood we are helping to make certain that they don't get broken in adolescence. And by allowing them failures in adolescence, we are helping to lay the groundwork for success in adulthood.*[6]

In addition, because immature adolescents tend to lack empathy, many of these teens do not experience some of the most significant consequences to their behavior—its impact on others. Yet, I've seen teens, whose parents are constantly excusing their bad decisions, exhibit a remarkable ability to manage their own behavior when they face limits within a significant relationship. When a teen is confronted by someone who really matters to him or her, and told to knock off certain behavior, it can lead to powerful changes in the teen's approach to life.

During the adolescent years, there is a tremendous amount of development in the regions of the brain that control and regulate impulses, feelings, and behavior.[7] The prefrontal cortex region, for example, is in the process of being wired in such a way that it allows a teen to effectively self-regulate. What's more, this important cortical wiring appears to be impacted by experience. As Dr. Daniel Siegel explains in his book, *The Developing Mind: How Relationships and the Brain Interact to Shape Who We Are*, children and teens appear to *require* assistance from significant others in their lives in order to develop the neural pathways that allow for effective self-regulation.[8] In other words, learning how to regulate impulses, emotions, and behavior occurs within the context of relationships. Perhaps that's why many teens who have relationship problems also have difficulties with self-regulatory functions.

For those teens who are delayed in developing self-regulatory functions, problems abound. They make very poor decisions that sometimes lead to serious consequences, such as legal trouble or expulsion from school. Levine notes that teens who have learned to self-regulate are at much less risk of substance abuse.[9] Those who have not developed important self-regulation skills are not only vulnerable to substance abuse and dependence, they also are prone to emotional outbursts and poor frustration tolerance because they lack the ability to regulate their emotional world. Many of these teens resort to maladaptive measures like cutting, self-harm, or drug abuse as a way of trying to cope with their tumultuous inner world.

Problems with Goal-Oriented Behavior

Immature teens tend to possess what McKinnon and Santa call a magical sense of the future. In other words, they lack an understanding of how the present connects to the future through a sequence of causes and effects. If they want to get into a good college, for example, they might grasp that getting good grades in high school is important, but they may not make the connection between completing homework assignments and getting good grades. In fact, it is often without any internal dissonance at all that they will refuse to do homework night after night and still insist that they can get into an ivy-league college. Immature teens will do what serves them best in the moment, without concern for future consequences.

In reality, their magical thinking is not only about the future. Immature teens lack the ability to connect past events with present realities. For example, when teens arrive at a wilderness camp, many of them experience a feeling of regret and, because of this, make promises to change. Once they begin to acknowledge the errors of their ways, they expect that the consequences should magically disappear and the behavior be forgiven. "I've changed," I hear them say to their parents. "I've learned my lesson. Now let me come home." Because this ploy has worked for them so often, they cannot accept that their past behavior has a present consequence that must be felt and experienced. These consequences can be positive or negative, depending on the action. However, immature teens are unable to orient their decision-making to future goals. Consequently, they flounder in the present, believing that all will be well in that magical future.

Teens who haven't practiced goal-oriented behavior typically will have little confidence in their abilities to achieve difficult goals. When challenges arise, they may bank on having someone bail them out, or they may quit prematurely. What they fail to develop in the process is an enduring sense of *self-efficacy* and *agency*, which Levine describes this way:

> *Self-efficacy is the belief that we can successfully impact our world ... When children are high in self-efficacy they find it easy to act on their own behalf. This ability to act appropriately in one's best interest is termed agency. Self-efficacy refers to beliefs; agency refers to actions; but they both refer to a sense of personal control.*[10]

Without experiences that prompt them to develop awareness of how their present decisions and actions affect their future, teens cannot *own* their lives. Instead, they remain dependent on others to orchestrate their future, which, more often than not, leads to high conflict with parents or whoever takes on the job of mapping out their lives. Teens who feel out of control are more likely to approach life like a helpless victim, never assuming responsibility for the consequences of their actions, and never understanding that they can only change the course of their lives through a series of goal-oriented choices.

Psychosocial Development

Psychosocial development occurs within the context of significant relationships over time. For young children, these relationships are usually with parents and family. As children grow older, they form other important relationships *in which* and *through which* they grow and mature. For teens, in particular, relationships with peers become extremely important

Short-sighted

Tricia was failing three classes in tenth grade. She was doing so because she would not complete her homework, and refused to study for tests. Even though Tricia's parents grounded her for failing, the punishment never produced any change. When she should have been studying, she would surf MySpace and instant-message her friends. When her parents took away the computer, she would text her friends on her cell phone. When they took away her cell phone, she would lie around listening to music. When I met Tricia, I asked her what she wanted to do with her life.

"I'm not sure – maybe be a veterinarian or a teacher or something."

"Interesting," I replied. *"So you are planning on going to college?"*

"Yes," she said, *"I can't be a vet or a teacher or anything without going to college!"*

"But you don't do your homework now. How will you get into college if you don't do your homework and fail your classes?"

"I don't know. I just will."

and influential, giving peers tremendous sway over one another's development. However, while these relationships may have a great impact on teens at various times, I believe that the enduring relationships they have with parents or primary caregivers continue to be of utmost importance in the child's emotional development.

The relationship between parents and child is a dynamic transaction of mutual influence that changes over time. By this, I mean that parents respond to the child's physical and emotional needs, and children respond to the parent's physical and emotional needs. However, most theories of parenting point to the need for adults to continually balance interactions with their child between *attunement*, on the one hand, and *containment* on the other. Attunement involves being attentive to a child and truly understanding her needs, her emotional climate, her communication strategies for expressing contentment or distress, and her capacities and limitations. Attuned responses to a child allow the child to "feel felt,"[11] which supplies a deep sense of being known and understood. Attunement is about seeing the child accurately and reflecting this awareness back to the child in a validating and nurturing way. It is akin to holding up a relationship-based mirror in which the child comes to know herself.

Attunement requires availability. You must be present with your child during her development in order to really "get" her and communicate your growing sense of who she is becoming. Attunement implies an awareness of how the child is evolving and of how she may need different responses to the same needs depending on where she is developmentally. For example, while a young toddler's angry outburst may be appropriately met with a soothing response from mom and willingness to retrieve the ball that the toddler threw into the next room, this would certainly not be the appropriate response to a kindergartner who screamed in rage after throwing his ball into the next room.

Attunement refers to a perceptive sensitivity to the child, particularly to his emotional state. We can also use terms such as nurturance, recognition, connection, and validation to describe this process. I prefer the term attunement, however, because it expresses how this very important developmental process works. A parent's attunement to a child promotes the child's ability to become attuned to himself, to become aware of his emotional state and the thoughts, beliefs and urges that accompany various states. As an adult, moment-by-moment attunement to one's experiences appears to be an indicator of emotional and relational health.[12]

Containment refers to the act of containing a child's experience through involved and attuned parental supervision. Just as a prenatal infant is contained within the womb of the mother, so, too, is a newborn's experience contained by the caregiver's attentive patterns of holding, rocking, and feeding. As children get older, containment by parents expands to include the attuned setting of limits. "No" is one of the most important words in an attuned parent's vocabulary. As children are growing and exploring their world, the parental "no" keeps them safe and provides a sense of security. Between ages two and five, the appropriate use of the word "no" teaches children that they are not the center of the universe, that there are limits to their involvement in their parents' lives and marriage, and that they have certain responsibilities as members of a social group, not the least of which is using the toilet. As they grow older, a parent's attuned application of limits helps develop children's sense of responsibility for schoolwork and encourages industriousness and determination. The questions that attuned parents ask throughout the child's development include: What is it that the child needs, wants, or feels right now? Who is responsible for this need, want, or feeling? What is a healthy balance of responsibility right now for my child's development?

Without limits, children do not grow up. Without limits held firmly and consistently, adolescents do not grow into mature young adults. Instead, they remain immature as they enter the school of hard knocks, which limits their behavior in ways that may lead to devastating consequences, such as jail, failed relationships, pink slips, or lifelong addictions.

Limit-setting challenges a child to grow in his understanding of who is responsible for his life. Limits not only teach him to tolerate frustration, but may motivate him to action. However, limits must be set and enforced within the context of a *significant relationship*. Limits without relationship create kids who may behave, but only to avoid punishment. This is why the boot camp approach does not work very well. The ideal consequence for ignoring limits is one that creates sufficient distress in the child, but not simply because she broke the rules. Consequences are most effective when they drive home the point that certain behavior negatively impacts those closest to you. Consequences should not be dealt out in an overly harsh and shaming manner. Instead, they should be clear in their purpose and backed by a resolve to enforce the limit in order to help the child mature.

Let me give you an example that illustrates this. Several years ago, I was working with a young man at a therapeutic boarding school. The holidays were approaching, and he was preparing for his first visit home to be with his family. The home visit had been a long time coming, as this young man had struggled to move forward in the therapeutic program. The family was so excited about his visit and had arranged for all their relatives to be there when he came home. However, two days before he was to leave for home, the young man was involved in underground activity that negatively impacted the entire student body. In response, his parents made one of the most impressive parenting decisions I have seen: They told him that he was not coming home for the holidays. This limit not only created distress for the boy, but his entire family agonized over the disappointment of not having him at home. But, they held firm, tolerated their own distress, and allowed the young man to deal with his unhappiness. Six months later, at his graduation, this young man and his family expressed that this was the turning point for him, as well as for their relationship.

In addition to limit-setting, containment involves supervising a child's experience. Obviously, parents cannot supervise all of a developing child's experiences, much less a teen's. But children need adults to be available and attentive to help them make sense of their experiences. They rely on parental judgment about certain experiences, even if they at times seem to resent parental supervision. With many of the struggling teens I meet, they have not received adequate supervision of their experiences. This is often a function of some rupture in their relationship with their parents, either a failure of attunement and connection, or a too permissive or too strict approach by their parents.

Why Developmental Delays Occur

How did we get here? This is the question so many parents want answered when they are faced with the realization that their teens are delayed in their psychosocial development. To be sure, there are a number of variables that may contribute to a delay in a child's development: traumatic experiences, family difficulties, stressful transitions, parental mental illness, or experiences of sickness or loss. Furthermore, a child's biological make-up can impede normal development. For our purposes, I'd like to focus on four common sources of developmental delay:

- Breakdowns in parent-child relationships
- Parents rescuing wayward teens
- Peer pressure
- Substance abuse

Breakdowns in the Parent-Child Relationship

Somewhere along the way, sometimes early on and sometimes much later, the relationship between the teens I work with and their parents or caregivers has broken down. Sometimes this breakdown occurs following a momentous event, such as parental divorce, or as the result of traumatic circumstances, such as parental abandonment or abuse. A trauma such as rape can also rupture the parent-child connection, when shame and secrecy undermine trust within the relationship. Sometimes relationships just deteriorate gradually, such as when children isolate themselves with a computer or gaming system and become increasingly resistant to parental authority and less attached to the parents. By the time teens' problems reach a crisis point, the relationship between them and their parents may carry little weight or influence. Sometimes, relationships are shattered by parental addiction or unavailability. Regardless of how a relationship breakdown occurs, the impact on a child's psychosocial development can be far-reaching. After all, children develop within the context of significant relationships.

At times, the parent-child relationship is intact, but the parents have not provided the necessary attunement and containment that the child needs from them. Breakdowns of this sort are very common in this age

Sly Gaming Addict

Another challenge to parental authority is that it is difficult for parents to enforce many limits. Immature teens often are incredibly sneaky and manipulative. Many are able to get around parental consequences.

I remember hearing one parent's story of how he and his wife were trying to limit their son's time on the computer because they were concerned about his addictive pattern of playing an online war game. First, they locked the room that contained the computer each night, turning the computer off so that a login was required to turn it back on. Then they installed a surveillance camera in the office. These parents meant business. Little did they know that their son had managed to make a copy of the office key. Each night, he would crawl into the office under a blanket and turn on the computer in such a way that it bypassed the need for a password. The boy then spent five to six hours playing the game, all the while leading his parents to believe they had successfully addressed his computer addiction.

of entitled children. As a result, many children struggle to accomplish the task of becoming mature young adults.

Many immature teens experience significant inconsistency in their parents' ability to be accurately attuned to them, while holding them to firm limits. Divorce or unresolved marital conflicts can contribute to this, such that the child is able to manipulate one parent against the other. I often tell parents that if they are not unified in their parenting approach, their child will play them. Children become quite adept at this game, and they typically can find their way around limits that are not imposed by a unified parental team.

In addition, teens often pay more attention to parental actions than words. If teens observe inconsistencies in their parents, they are less likely to accept their authority. "Do as I say, not as I do" is not a good mantra for effective parenting. On the flip side, too many parents I work with feel that they must constantly justify their limits to the children. They seem to assume that kids must be part of a democratic process of limit-setting. In this way, many parents give up their parental authority because of their personal conflicts about limit setting.

Tendency to Rescue Teens from Consequences

Another disturbing pattern I see in teen-parent relationships is an unwillingness among many parents to allow their child to face the natural consequences of bad behavior. Over and over again, these parents rescue their children, sheltering them from what may be the very thing that would be most helpful to them. Teens certainly encourage this, manipulating their parents by grousing about the injustice of limits or consequences, by lying about being wrongfully accused, or by feigning remorse and admitting they made a stupid, impulsive decision.

It's easy to understand why parents want to ride to the rescue. The consequences facing many immature teens are often of very serious magnitude. Many are in legal hot water. Others are failing classes and messing up their chances for getting into college. Some are engaging in activities that could destroy their parents' property or deplete their bank accounts. Others are teetering on the edge of addiction. And no small number of immature teens are at risk of sinking so low into the quagmire of their failing adolescence that suicide seems like a viable option to them.

However, if parents are to change the trajectory of their teens' current paths, instead of bailing them out, they may need to change teens' environment so that they can face the natural consequences of an immature approach to life, while avoiding the most devastating effects. These teens may require an environment where they can be free from the many negative influences and distractions that keep them from doing the necessary work of growing up and learning from poor decisions. They will need a healthier peer group, from whom they will receive support and reinforcement for making more mature decisions.

The Peer Group

Teens are more invested in their peer relationships than they are in their relationships with parents and families.[13] It is within these relationships that teens are learning how to approach life's daily challenges. Unfortunately, most peer groups tend to lack any commitment to mature ways of approaching life and relationships. Of course, this is not always the case. Some adolescents find themselves connected to a group of friends who are successfully facing the demands of being a teenager. These adolescents tend to ascribe to the norms of the group, and may demonstrate impressive motivation to prepare for a successful future. These kids usually are concerned about how their behavior impacts others, displaying a healthy respect for social order. When I was a teen, I found myself involved with just such a group. It was seeing the attention most of them gave to their schoolwork that motivated me to place a priority on studying and preparing for college.

Unfortunately, most of the teens with whom I work, illustrate the saying: "Birds of a feather flock together." Floundering teens more often than not befriend other floundering teens. And do not underestimate the power of this association. What often happens is that these teens alienate themselves from anyone who approaches life differently, including their parents. And they become incredibly loyal to their peer group. Despite numerous parental lectures, attempts by parents to spend time with them, and even the weekly therapy sessions they are forced to attend, they remain unwavering in their commitment to the peer group. Often, they find the acceptance that they crave from peers, and until they are either removed from those peers, or the group itself experiences some kind of disruption, they will remain loyal regardless of the consequences.

The Prevalence of Substance Abuse

Drugs are prolific amongst today's teens. A 12-year-old boy recently shared with me that if he wanted to fit in at his school, he either had to smoke pot, be a jock, or be a nerd. By high school, of course, teens are regularly exposed to harder drugs than marijuana and alcohol. Some pop ADHD pills or their parent's pain pills between classes, consume shrooms on the weekends, and almost certainly know of other students who are using ecstasy, cocaine, methamphetamine, or heroin.

There are a number of risks associated with teen drug use. I don't want to go through all of them here, but I do want to point out some of the key ways substances impact development. First, substances can negatively affect the development of brain cells. Second, drug use may keep immature teens from benefiting from their experiences in dealing with the frustrations in relationships. Substances numb those frustrations and lead users to disconnect themselves from important relationships that do not support their drug habit. Parental relationships are often the first to go, though some teens mask it well by pretending compliance and respect, while leading a secret, second life.

In Summary

The teens I meet are not just a collection of symptoms. It's true that many of them share common struggles—depression, anxiety, oppositional behavior, eating disorders, self-destructive habits, substance abuse—but most are also suffering from various aspects of developmental delay syndrome, as evidenced in their immaturity in relationships, self-regulation, and goal-oriented behavior.

For these teens, therapeutic schools and programs may be just the place where they can safely grow up, where they can get the environmental and relational experiences that will put them on the path to healthy development. Therapeutic schools and programs are a good alternative to outpatient therapy and medical interventions because they are structured so that distractions are limited or removed, creating an environment where teens can interact with attentive adults who are available for forming relationships based on mutual respect and trust. Under the supervision of attuned adults, therapeutic programs nurture a peer culture where teens begin to own and enforce positive community expectations and values amongst themselves.

In the next two chapters, I'll provide an overview of therapeutic programs and the typical sequence for moving through them. I will also describe what to expect should you decide that this is an appropriate intervention for you and your teen.

[1] Kegan, Robert. *In Over Our Head: the Mental Demands of Modern Life*. (Cambridge: Harvard University Press, 1994).

[2] Santa, J. Leadership Award Address. Presented at the conference of the National Association of Therapeutic Schools and Programs, La Jolla, California. (January, 2007).

[3] Kohut, H. *The Analysis of the Self*. (New York: International Universities Press, 1971).

[4] Levine, M. *The Price of Privilege: How parental pressure and material advantage are creating a generation of disconnected and unhappy kids*. (New York: Harper Collins, 2006).

[5] Siegel, D. J. *The Developing Mind: How Relationships and the Brain Interact to Shape Who We Are*. (New York: Guilford, 1999).

[6] Levine, 79.

[7] Walsh, D. *Why Do They Act That Way? A Survival Guide to the Adolescent Brain for You and Your Teen*. (New York: Guilford, 2004).

[8] Siegel, D. J.

[9] Levine, M.

[10] Levine, 80.

[11] Siegel, D. J. and M. Hartzell. *Parenting from the Inside Out: How a Deeper Self-Understanding can help you raise children who thrive*. (New York: Penquin, 2004).

[12] Siegel, D. J. and M. Hartzell

[13] Taffel, R. *Breaking through to Teens: A new psychotherapy for the new adolescence*. (New York: Guilford, 2005).

CHAPTER THREE

CHOOSING A RESIDENTIAL PROGRAM

How do you find a place where your teen will succeed?

Residential treatment programs can help struggling and immature teens move forward in their development in the realms of relationships, self-regulation, and goal-oriented behavior, even where other interventions have failed. So what does an effective program look like? First, residential programs should provide a nurturing community where students are surrounded by attuned, attentive adults. Second, residential programs should be a place where teens will have positive social experiences with their peers. Third, residential programs should create an environment where students are unplugged from the distractions that are interfering with their ability to grow and develop. Let's look briefly at why each of these factors is so important.

A Community of Relationships

Once again, let me repeat what I believe is at the heart of our discussion here: Psychosocial development, or the process of growing up and approaching life and relationships in healthy, mature ways, occurs within the context of significant relationships. Among the most important of these, of course, is the parent-child relationship, which, at its best, provides a developing child with a proper balance of attuned parenting and containment. However, when teens are stuck in their development or delayed in some important and significant way, it is my opinion that they also must develop significant relationships with adults and peers who will encourage their growth and maturity. Medications may play a part in the process, but medications alone cannot bring about the kind of growth and maturity that will enable teens to be more successful in their lives and relationships.

Teens need relationships with adults who are available to them, who notice them, who are attuned to their moods, who listen to and appreciate their opinions, but who also are willing to challenge them at appropriate times. Teens need to form bonds with adults who supervise them—who know where they are, who they're with, and what they're up to—and who consistently limit experiences that may derail the teens' development or injure them in some way. Teens need to connect with adults who they can come to respect and identify with, whose opinions will matter to them. They need to know that these adults are watching out for them, assisting them in the process of growing up, and helping them to make sense of their experiences.

Teens also need relationships with peers who are themselves in the process of growing up. Because teens place such a high value on peer relationships during their adolescence, these relationships need to be supervised and contained within a community of attuned adults, who uphold limits that are relatively consistent. Without this supervision, immature teens will form peer groups that support their shared immature approach to life and relationships.

Freedom from Distractions

In order to progress in their psychosocial development, most struggling teens need time away from the distractions that are keeping them from participating in significant relationships. In other words, teens need limits on the amount of time they can access the Internet, sit in front of a video game or a television, talk or text on cell phones, and listen to iPods. The distractions of alcohol and drugs need to be removed as well. Teens who have poor judgment or who lack realistic expectations for the future are not well-equipped to engage in typical teen exploration. These immature teens cannot adequately regulate substance use and are therefore at risk of many negative consequences. Similarly, mind-altering substances may severely inhibit their ability to form beneficial significant relationships in the community.

Therapeutic schools and programs remove or seriously limit many of these distractions. They also create a community of engaged and attuned adults who provide containment and limits for the teens. This environment allows a positive peer culture to develop, which can be one of the most important factors in helping struggling teens to grow up. While parents may worry that there aren't enough distractions available in residential programs, the reality is that teens in these positive communities tend to be happier and more connected than ever before.

Moving Forward with Development

When struggling teens are connected to a positive community with clear rules and expectations, they are able to move forward with developmental tasks. They begin to evolve a clear and consistent identity within a community that knows them, attends to them, and supports them. They begin to own their lives and understand not only that they are responsible for their actions, but that their actions connect to the future in a logical, sequential way. They begin to learn effective ways to regulate their impulses, to identify and express their emotional states, and to anticipate the impact their actions might have on their future and their relationships. They also come to realize that they have an obligation to their community to uphold its values and norms.

In short, although many teens arrive at therapeutic programs *behind* in their psychosocial development, what I have observed time and time again is that they complete such programs functioning *more maturely* than many of their peers back home.

The Right Fit for Your Child

If you are serious about sending your child to a therapeutic school or program, it's critical that you understand the ins and outs of selecting a program and enrolling your child. Some of you, of course, may already be engaged in this process. Others of you, however, may know very little about these kinds of therapeutic programs and schools. Indeed, prior to my becoming a therapist at a therapeutic school, I also knew very little about the different types of programs and schools available. Choosing the right program can certainly be daunting for parents, especially in a moment of crisis, when decisions must be made quickly.

Not everyone will experience the same process when they decide to send their child to a residential program; however, most families tend to take similar paths on this journey. For instance, in my years of working in a wilderness program and a therapeutic boarding school, I have observed that many teens initially attend a short-term wilderness program (usually lasting 4–12 weeks), and then go on to a therapeutic school immediately afterwards (usually for 8–24 months, depending on the school and the needs of the child). Table 3.1 presents this typical sequence.

The Crisis Point

By the time parents begin to consider an intensive intervention that involves sending their kids away, they typically have tried numerous strategies to get their sons or daughters to change. However, these struggling teens usually deny that they have a problem. Their problems, as they see them, come from the outside, not the inside. They blame their idiotic parents, their incompetent teachers, or the fact that all of their friends are doing the *same* things they are. They simply are not aware that their approach to life is ineffective. They believe the world around them should change, and they are often oblivious to the idea that they should be making better decisions. Kegan describes this as being "embedded" in an approach.[1] It is not that they necessarily choose to act entitled and narcissistic—they just don't yet realize there is another way. Narcissistic and entitled is often what they *are*, not just how they *act*. The immature approach to their lives is, at this moment, not up for discussion because they cannot see their behavior in an objective or reflective way.

Because of this, parents often have to make decisions about their teens without their involvement. This flies in the face of a parenting culture that believes all decisions should be democratic ones, and that the teen should consent to any limit the parents set. This is absurd, really. These teens have been clearly demonstrating that they lack mature judgment for solving their problems or managing their lives. One of the important changes within the family system that often needs to occur is the restoration of parental authority. Teens need their parents to understand what "the big picture" looks like for them, as they are simply unable to see it. Certainly, the majority of struggling teens will not initially be able to see the benefit of going to a therapeutic school or program.

Engaging an Educational Consultant

It is normally after a crisis that parents enlist the services of an educational consultant. Educational consultants are professionals who are trained to assist families in identifying appropriate educational placements for children who are struggling with learning and/or emotional and behavioral challenges. I believe their expertise is invaluable, and I strongly urge you, if you have not already, to seek the help of an educational consultant who is familiar with therapeutic schools and programs to help you select the right placement for your child. A good resource to begin this search is the Independent Educational Consultants Association (IECA). Its website is *www.educationalconsulting.org*. School counselors also may be able to refer you to a consultant in your area.

Some families start their search for therapeutic schools or programs on the Internet, exploring websites for different programs in lieu of retaining the services of an educational consultant. Parents, please be careful about this. I have looked at many websites for programs across the country, and some of the best programs unfortunately have the worst websites, while some of the less reputable programs have websites that glitter and paint an image of quality. Sending your child to a residential program will be a life-altering experience for you and your teen, and it's not

Table 3.1
The Typical Sequence of Treatment

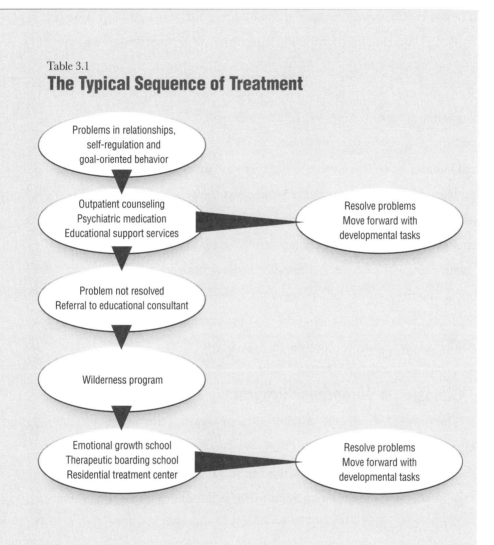

a decision you should make without expert guidance. Although I wish I could tell you that all therapeutic programs are reputable and capable of getting your child back on the right path, obviously that is not the case. And, you may not be able to ascertain from the website whether or not a particular program is a good fit for your teen.

Depending on the nature and severity of an adolescent's problems, educational consultants generally advise a sequence of interventions to address the problematic behaviors and the family and social dynamics that are hindering the child's academic and/or psychological development. For teens who are defiant and resist acknowledging that their approach to life is a problem, or for those who need observation and evaluation to determine what the best intervention might be, going to a wilderness program is often the first step.

Choosing a Wilderness Program

The process of selecting a wilderness program is not a casual undertaking. At the risk of sounding like a broken record, I want to emphasize how immensely important it is for you to receive guidance from an experienced educational consultant who is familiar with various wilderness programs and who can help you select one that is a good fit for your child. In my experience, many educational consultants refer teens to particular programs based on the clinical expertise of the therapists practicing at that program. Often, they will refer you directly to a particular therapist who has demonstrated expertise in effectively addressing the problems that your teen may be presenting.

Choosing an Educational Consultant

1. Look for a consultant who has expertise in working with children with emotional and/or behavioral problems, and who has made successful placements in special needs facilities or residential programs.

2. Ask your physician, therapist, or school counselor for referrals. If they cannot provide any, you can find consultants affiliated with the Independent Educational Consultants Association (IECA) at *www.educationalconsulting.org*.

3. Consultants do not always need to meet with your child, especially if the child is defiant and resistant to treatment. However, the consultant should obtain a thorough history of the child's problems from you or other caregivers. They should also review the child's previous psychological or educational evaluations.

4. Consultants should demonstrate an understanding of both the academic needs of your child and the emotional and behavioral needs. Do they seem to really "get" your child?

5. Evaluate your comfort level with the consultant after you've met with him or her. It is very important that you have trust and confidence in the consultant's ability to help you and your child.

6. Ask the educational consultant: "What can we gain from working with you?" He or she should be able to explain the process you are about to undertake and what to expect as you begin to address your child's difficulties.

As I mentioned in the introduction, therapeutic wilderness programs are not the same as boot camps or military schools. The wilderness programs that I am describing emphasize humane, evidence-based therapy that focuses on positive behavioral change. These programs do not emphasize discipline or harsh and punitive confrontation.

Another thing for you to consider as you weigh your options is the accreditation or professional affiliations of the wilderness program. Look for programs that are accredited by The Joint Commission, the premier accrediting agency for U.S. hospitals and healthcare facilities, or for those associated with the Outdoor Behavioral Healthcare Industry Council (OBHIC) or the National Association of Therapeutic Schools and Programs (NATSAP). Also, check the state licensing of the program, as well as the licenses and credentials of the clinicians.

You will also want to ask about the typical number of teens in each group. I recommend group sizes be no larger than 11 or 12, and ideally between 7–10 students. Also, the staff to student ratio should be no larger than 1:3. This ensures that students receive adequate attention from their designated staff members.

Find out how often your child will meet with his or her therapist, and who will be carrying out the treatment when the therapist is not present. In addition, you should inquire if a psychologist will be conducting a comprehensive psychological evaluation of your teen. This is often necessary in determining appropriate next steps in your teen's treatment.

Finally, always ask for references of parents whose children have completed the wilderness program. Ask questions about how their child was kept safe.

A Snapshot of the Wilderness Camp Experience

Wilderness therapy programs use different methods to create a growth environment for participants. For example, some have base camps, where students spend time between periodic treks into the wilderness. Others keep students in the wilderness setting for the duration of their stay, allowing the groups to set up their own camps throughout their sojourn and teaching them the principles of "Leave No Trace" camp-

Questions of Safety

If you are thinking about a wilderness program, you undoubtedly have safety concerns. A well-run program will welcome your questions. If you're not sure what questions to ask, start with these:

- Are students regularly seen by a physician to monitor their health? If so, how often?

- How are routine physical complaints such as nausea, blisters, or muscle pain managed?

- How do program employees monitor participants' ongoing physical health? (For example, are there regular foot checks?)

- Are students educated about sanitizing hands, cooking and eating utensils? How are they monitored?

- What are the procedures for managing a crisis? Do group leaders have a way to make immediate contact with base? Can a student be evacuated if necessary?

- Are field staff trained in First Aid, CPR, or Wilderness First Responder?

- How do staff manage extreme weather conditions?

- What are the possible risks for a teen in a particular wilderness program (e.g., heat exhaustion, snakebite, hiking injuries, etc.), and how are these managed?

- How is water and food kept safe?

ing. I prefer the latter because I think it provides a more intensive learning experience for teens, but I believe effective work can be carried out through both models.

The essence of the wilderness experience is for teens to be imbedded in a natural environment that is free from the many distractions and comforts that have prevented them from developing a mature, realistic understanding of their world. Nature is not easily manipulated, and this realization ultimately brings teens face to face with the maladaptive methods they've been using to control their parents, their peers, and themselves. Living in the wild is an unfamiliar experience for most teens, which may make them feel unsettled and uncomfortable. However, under the care of trained and compassionate field instructors, teens use their wilderness experiences to draw parallels to their "real world" lives. As therapists interact with troubled teens in these settings, they get a clear and natural assessment of the teens' coping strategies and beliefs. This enables the therapist to help these teens make positive changes in their approach to life.

A typical day in the wilderness involves a group of teens doing a series of tasks that must be accomplished by working together. This includes preparing and cleaning up after meals, organizing their belongings to ensure that they are well taken care of and protected from the elements, and managing their campsites to minimize their impact to the environment. All of these processes provide numerous opportunities for teens to learn about themselves and each other, and there are moments of feedback and reflection throughout the day.

The groups also hike on a regular basis. These hikes challenge and reward teens at many levels: They get practice in tolerating frustration; they learn how to offer and receive support and encouragement, and feel their confidence building as they accomplish difficult tasks and experience the joy of reaching their destination. And, always, their counselors are making sure that the teens see how their experiences are metaphorically tied back to the "real world" so that important life principles are recognized and reinforced.

Homeward bound? Not so fast!

Once teens finish their wilderness program, most believe they are ready to come home, and they will try to convince their parents that they have turned the corner. However, in my experience, the majority of kids coming out of the wilderness have not yet internalized the changes needed for them to succeed when they get back to their old stomping grounds.

I encourage parents to work with their child's wilderness therapist and educational consultant while the child is in the wilderness to determine whether returning home after wilderness is a viable option. Frequently, it is not. However, there are a number of factors to consider, and I have seen occasions where teens had the emotional maturity needed to make returning home an option. For most, though, the best next step is a residential therapeutic school.

Finding the Right Therapeutic School

Therapeutic schools provide a long-term residential setting where teens can attain academic credit towards a diploma, while also living in a community that is organized to promote growth and development. Students at therapeutic schools often live in an environment where they will be shielded from the many distractions that bombard them at home. This setting makes it easier for them to focus on self-development, growth in relationships, adherence to established community norms, and support for mature and effective decision-making.

Therapeutic schools use a variety of models for educating and treating kids, and most specialize in working with children who have specific types of problems. Schools may be single-sex or co-ed, with student bodies ranging from very small to quite large.

Some other differences between schools include:

- **Amount of structure**. Schools may range from tightly secured facilities to campuses that allow teens some freedom to come and go.
- **Balance of therapeutic and academic programming**. At one end are residential treatment centers that strongly emphasize therapeutic activities, at the other end are "emotional growth schools," which weave therapeutic programming into a primarily academically oriented program.
- **Clinical sophistication of the staff**. Some schools employ doctoral level psychologists, who work in tandem with a psychiatrist to oversee the therapeutic programming, while others may only contract with therapists or psychiatrists in their community, who meet with the kids on an "as needed" basis.
- **Treatment models**. The focus may be on individual and group therapy or on the "therapeutic milieu," which is the social environment where psychosocial growth occurs.
- **Duration of the program**.
- **Cost**.

Whether the school provides intensive individual and group therapy or provides therapeutic intervention by creating a positive peer culture, teens in these facilities are constantly challenged to appraise themselves honestly and to evaluate how well they are managing the demands of their lives.

Many of the teens who enroll in therapeutic schools have struggled with problems such as depression, anxiety, defiance of authority, low self-esteem, eating disorders, poor anger management, self-destructive behaviors, and substance abuse. Many also have learning issues; some are related to a cognitive deficit, others are simply the result of lack of effort. Therapeutic schools are set up to deal with all of these of issues and to address the immature approach that so many of these teens employ.

As you investigate therapeutic schools or programs, here are some tips from the National Association of Therapeutic Schools and Programs (*www.natsap.org*) for you and your educational consultant:

- **Verify the licensure or accreditation of the facility**. If they are not licensed or accredited, they should be able to articulate reasons they are not. For example, some states do not have appropriate licensure categories for therapeutic schools or residences, or in some states, the program is better described as a private school than as a treatment program. They should also be able to describe the process they use to evaluate the work they do. A list of accrediting agencies can be found at www.natsap.org.
- **Confirm the licensure of the clinical or therapy staff**. If the state in which the program resides does not require licensure, it is important to research the credentials of the staff. Verify the credentials are appropriate to the treatment they propose to offer; e.g. if they have individual or group therapy, is it provided by individuals with appropriate advance degrees (MSW, LCSW, Ph.D. MD, etc.)?
- **Verify that the academic curriculum is accredited by a recognized academic accrediting body**. Are the teachers qualified by credential or experience to teach the courses the school or program offers?
- **If counseling is offered, is it provided by staff who are full-time employees of the program or is it provided by adjunct or independent personnel?** If the latter,

is the cost included in the program's tuition or is there an additional fee for this service?

- **Obtain multiple sources of information about the program or school prior to enrollment**. For example, you can ask for references from past clients, obtain the recommendation of a professional educational consultant and, if at all possible, visit the program or school to determine if you are comfortable with the environment, culture, methods employed, and general assessment of staff, students and climate of the school.

- **If you visit the program or school, ask to speak to current students without staff present, and ask the students what their experience is like**. Ask each student what they have gained from the program, what they like the most and what they like the least.

- **Inquire about outcomes**. There is little good data on outcome, but ask what efforts the program has made to assess how they are doing and to improve their performance. Ask how they assess student improvement and determine readiness for advancement or graduation.

- **Ask for an estimate of program length and what factors determine readiness to complete the program**.

- **Ask about the program's philosophy of change and methods of discipline**.

- **Ask what is expected of families**. Family involvement is an important factor at all NATSAP member schools and programs. It is an essential component of your child's recovery process. Therefore, we recommend that, no matter what your choice, ensure that family involvement is a key part of the program.

- **Ask about any restrictions on family communication and visitation**.

- **Ask for a description of the program's "levels" or stages of progress**. Most programs have a "level" system or series of steps in the program that determine progress and privileges.

■ **Understand that there is a long continuum of care for struggling children**. Any particular program is usually just one step in a long process of helping a child mature and address the emotional, psychological, and behavioral problems that lead to residential placement.

It is beyond the scope of this book to describe all the different programs available, or to recommend certain types over others. That's why I believe your best guide is an educational consultant who is very familiar with the schools and programs that treat children like yours. However, once your consultant makes a recommendation, don't make a decision before visiting the prospective school to meet the staff who will be caring for your child, as well as some of the students. Remember, you are selecting a village, a place to provide the structure and support that your child needs while he acquires the necessary experiences to mature and get back on track in his life.

[1] Kegan, R. *The Evolving Self: Problem and Process in Human Development.* (Cambridge: Harvard University Press, 1991).

CHAPTER FOUR

ADOLESCENCE UNPLUGGED

What's it like to go to a wilderness program?

People have been retreating to the wilderness for thousands of years, pursuing spiritual and psychological renewal. It is a place removed from the distractions and cultural temptations of daily life. It's a place where religious ascetics, students of various spiritual traditions, and society's outcasts alike go to wrestle with issues of meaning and purpose, to challenge themselves in harsh and demanding conditions, or to complete some rite of passage that pushes the boundaries of human potential. One of the most important benefits of going through a wilderness experience is that it provides an opportunity to step out of the familiar, to reflect on one's experiences, and to gain insight about problems in living.

In the last 20 years, the wilderness also has become a therapeutic resource for those seeking to help struggling teens who have not responded to outpatient treatment or who have refused to comply with their parents' limits. For many of these teens, the wilderness experience provides an unparalleled learning opportunity and multiple therapeutic benefits. Before we look at those benefits, I'd like to share an excerpt from a letter a mom sent to her 17-year-old son soon after he arrived in the woods. I believe it captures the essence of what is wonderful about the wilderness experience.

Letter from Mom

Dear Tommy:

It sounds like you are really in the wilderness. Sometimes we need to be in the wilderness to understand what really matters in life. I think we go to the wilderness a lot in life at different times. Sometimes, these are times of pain and loss, and sometimes these are times of growth and enlightenment. I know this time for you will probably involve all those feelings and experiences. Sometimes we just don't know what we got till it's gone, and sometimes the wilderness will make it all clear to us. I have had dark days of the soul as every human will, and I can honestly say I have learned and become a better person through going through every one of those moments. I know you will, too.

I am so happy and proud of you for recognizing and owning up to the mistakes you have made. Everybody on earth recognizes things about themselves they want to change, things they want to improve in order to be a better person, and so they can make a positive impact upon our world. I hear you saying you are recognizing these things and you are ready to accept the challenge. I know you and I believe in you. So as uncomfortable and unhappy as you are sometimes, know that you are doing important work and going through a very important time. Sometimes, we need to be in the wilderness to know how blessed it is to be in the land of milk and honey. I love you and I am here for you, praying for your strength when you need it.

Love,
Mom

Going to wilderness

Once you commit to sending your child to a wilderness program, you must decide how to get him or her there. Some teens go willingly, and you or friends can transport them. However, for many families, the decision to send their child to a wilderness program is made during a crisis, when there is significant tension in the parent-child relationship. In such situations, teens are often volatile and unwilling to comply with their parents' requests. If that happens, you may be advised to hire professionals to transport your child to the wilderness program. A number of reputable transport companies provide this service for parents. I recommend hiring an educational consultant to guide you in these decisions. Generally, consultants advise parents not to tell their teen they are being sent to wilderness until the transporters arrive, usually in the early morning hours. Parents then inform the child about where they are going, and why it is necessary. The transporters will take over the job of managing the adolescent at that point.

This experience can be extremely difficult and emotional for parents. It is a leap of faith and trust to hand your child over to the transporters. Most often, when teens meet the transporters, who are trained and able to manage this situation with a gentle, but firm approach, they accept the situation and comply, although sometimes with displays of reluctance and emotion. A few teens, however, are so non-compliant and so manipulative that they may hurl threats and insults at their parents as they are taken away kicking and screaming.

Let me emphasize that transporting your child to the wilderness is often the most emotionally charged part of the process, even for those who have accepted the need for such a drastic intervention. Manipulative teens can and will play on parents' emotional vulnerability. One couple, for example, tearfully described watching their teenaged son struggle with the escorts, while screaming obscenities and personal attacks at them. This is a moment of tough love, and it requires tough resolve on the part of parents.

Using Transport Companies

- Necessary if child is unwilling to cooperate with parental decision that a wilderness program or therapeutic school is needed, or if there is concern that the child will run away, become volatile, or engage in dangerous behavior like a drug binge.
- Choose a reputable company and check references from other parents who have used them.
- Do not lie to your child about where he is are going. Be clear and specific, insisting that you are sending him to a therapeutic program to help him.
- In most cases, parents should be present when transport company arrives to get their child.

In these circumstances, it's important to remember that firm limits are necessary to push teens toward maturity. Standing by the decision to limit your teen's freedom sends the message loud and clear that the rules of the game have changed. Bad behavior and immature responses to problems will no longer be tolerated, and you unequivocally mean it!

A Wake Up Call

Sending teens to a wilderness program hits the pause button on their lives and gets their attention. It helps adolescents begin to understand that something is seriously wrong with their approach to life, and that it's time for them to take a good hard look at themselves and take responsibility for making necessary changes. I've seen a number of kids arrive in the woods with their backpacks on and a dawning awareness that life as they know it has stopped. The distractions and maladaptive coping patterns that they have relied on to avoid dealing with their problems are unavailable or rendered useless. They are face to face with firm limits in a place with no computers, no cell phones, no iPods, no drugs, and none of the comforts they have so often taken for granted. Initially, most will try to manipulate their parents to get them out of this situation, but their parents have already been warned that it is imperative that those manipulations fall on deaf ears.

Teens arrive at wilderness programs expressing mixed emotions. Some are bewildered and amazed that their parents set such a firm limit. Some are pissed off, others are anxious. Regardless of their emotional state, they are met by a calm, caring staff, who will support them and teach them how to care for themselves, but who will not rescue them from feeling whatever it is they need to feel. Indeed, it is very important that they experience a full range of emotions at this time, as distress and discomfort are often the necessary fuel to spark change.

One of the most important objectives in the wilderness is to get these kids to wake up to the impact of their behavior on themselves and others. They are challenged to develop empathy for others by confronting how they have disregarded and disrespected their parents and family, even if it was unintentional.

Living with Natural Consequences

In the wilderness, kids are able to experience immediate connections between their decisions and behavior and the consequences that follow. Remember, one of the hallmarks of an immature approach is the belief that one is immune to natural consequences, a mindset that actually keeps kids from developing any interest in regulating their impulses. Many of the teens I meet in the wilderness have been rescued so often by their parents that it's no surprise they feel immune to negative consequences. As Levine notes *in The Price of Privilege*, rescuing parents mean well, but they are actually hindering their child's development of self-efficacy and self-confidence.[1]

Life in the wilderness requires intention and consideration for the consequences of each action or non-action. Teens begin to understand that there's a connection between present and future, and that, even though many variables are out of their control, such as weather or other people's behavior, their responses do exert some control over what happens in the immediate and even the distant future.

The wilderness provides a safe container for teens to learn this invaluable lesson. While the consequences of making mistakes in the wilderness can certainly be unpleasant—a wet sleeping bag from being exposed to the rain, or diarrhea from not properly sanitizing hands or eating utensils—they are not nearly as devastating as the consequences that await many of these teens in the "real world." Arrests, school failure, or a drug overdose are a few of the consequences that many of these struggling teens are at risk for, if they have not already experienced them. Natural consequences are the great teacher. I will often tell kids when they arrive in the wilderness that it is the wilderness that is the therapist here, and that my job is to help them learn about themselves as they function with a group to manage the challenges of living in the wild.

A new social experience

Because adolescents are so highly influenced by their peer group, wilderness therapy programs and most therapeutic schools utilize the peer group to confront the teens' problematic approaches and to support them as they learn more mature ways of dealing with their experiences. The impact of this type of "milieu" approach is powerful. And the wilderness setting itself provides a unique opportunity for creating a social experience for teens that is unlike any others they've known.

First of all, the wilderness is the great equalizer. It does not matter what kind of clothes they wear, how much money their family has, or even what kinds of things they are into. Teens in wilderness find themselves all in the same boat, facing the same daily challenges, dependent on each other if they want the group to function well. The wilderness strips away the masks that teens hide behind, so that they see themselves more realistically as they are reflected in the eyes of their peers.

Sometimes parents express anxiety about the kinds of kids that might be in their child's group. While this concern is something that must be managed and addressed by wilderness professionals, I most often observe that teens often find they have much in common, even when their lifestyles, histories and presenting issues appear to be vastly different. This realization opens the door for them to develop empathy.

Second, wilderness programs are structured to create and maintain a social milieu that promotes healthy problem-solving and effective communication of feelings, needs, and wants. Over time, the peer group begins to hold members accountable for their behavior, confronting those within the group who refuse to adopt the group's norms or expectations. As teens progress through the program, some will assume leadership roles in their group. For many, this will be the first experience they have ever had in the role of a *positive* leader.

Third, being part of a tight-knit, interdependent group that must work together to accomplish tasks, often mimics the family experience. Teens tend to adopt roles that are familiar, and this provides an excellent opportunity for them to gain awareness of how they contribute to the dynamics in their family-of-origin. For example, Julie has a pattern in her family of shutting down and withdrawing whenever there is conflict. This not only serves to help her avoid the conflict, but it also causes family members to over-function on her behalf, to have to intuit what she needs, to treat her very sensitively, and to lower their expectations of her. As Julie begins to play out this dynamic in the peer group, she is confronted by peers who refuse to shield her from her obligations. What's more, they also expect her to speak up and be engaged in the process of resolving conflict within the group.

A Time for Assessment

Wilderness programs increasingly are becoming a precursor for teens headed to therapeutic schools. One of the major reasons is that these programs provide an excellent opportunity for therapists to assess the personalities and needs of adolescents and their families. Observing adolescents in a wilderness environment for a couple of months allows therapists and staff to get a clear picture of how they cope with difficulties and stress, how they function in a group environment, and how rigid or flexible they are to trying new approaches. For those teens who have been abusing substances, it allows an opportunity to assess them while they are free from the effects of drugs or alcohol.

Many therapeutic schools rely on the wilderness therapists to ascertain the nature of the adolescent's core struggles and to determine what level of structure might be necessary to address those issues adequately. These assessments are a very important step in finding the best fit for an adolescent among various therapeutic schools. In their evaluations, therapists look at things like psychological mindedness, openness to confrontation, motivation for change, behavior management problems, rigidity of approach, cognitive processing, as well as the presence of addictions or other serious psychological disturbances. Parent variables that tend to be important in the evaluative process include the parents' investment in the process, their willingness to cooperate with the treatment, their emotional availability, their commitment to upholding firm limits and staying the course of treatment, and any factors that may promote or inhibit the teen's therapeutic work. Such factors include parental mental illness; marital conflict, discord, or divorce; and other life circumstances that could affect the treatment process.

Preparing for Change

The ultimate goal of the wilderness experience is to help adolescents and their families better understand the nature of the child's problem and to prepare him to engage in the process of change. Having worked in a therapeutic school, I know first-hand how beneficial it is for a therapist to receive an adolescent from a wilderness program who is beginning to understand he has a problematic approach to life and who has shown some motivation to change. In contrast, those students who come directly to therapeutic schools, without first attending a wilderness program, generally will not hit the ground running. Instead, they often spend several months in the program refusing to engage in the process or to demonstrate any desire to change. They often fight with parents and program staff about the necessity for treatment, and many are not willing to accept the feedback of either their peer group or therapists.

To prepare kids for change, the metaphorical tool we use in the wilderness is a mirror. As teens face the daily demands and challenges, therapists will continually hold up a mirror, so adolescents can see more clearly how their approach plays out in daily experience. We cut away at denial, gradually leading teens to own their problems. This experience of being seen accurately and confronted within the context of relation-ships is one that struggling teens have not encountered consistently.

As time passes and teens accept the fact that their parents are not go-ing to rescue them, an amazing shift occurs in their attitude. By the end of their stint in the wilderness, most teens appear to have made some important progress. Parents are often amazed by their child's new, softer attitude. One parent, upon reuniting with her son after he completed a wilderness session, said to me with a proud relief: "He found his smile again—I feel like I have my son back."

Let me offer a word of caution here. Experiences like seeing the smile on a child's face are wonderful moments for celebration and relief. However, in my experience, these moments may not signal that the child is ready to go home. Many parents desperately want to bring their children home at this point and forego the continued work to be done at a therapeutic school. I have watched a number of well-meaning parents take their son and daughter home at this point only to call me later and report that the teen had slipped back into familiar, negative patterns and an immature *modus operandi*. The fact is that the improvements at this point are actually due to the teens being immersed in an environment that promotes and supports their progress. In other words, their change in attitude and behavior is best attributed to the program structure, or the therapeutic environment. For many, their gains have not yet become internalized such that they can maintain them in an environment that is not structured to support those changes.

Dan exemplifies this point. His mom had sent him to the wilderness program where I was working, and he did quite well in his eight weeks there. So his mom decided to bring him home, despite my cautions. She worked hard to structure their home environment, to set up counseling for her and her son, and to arrange tutoring. Unfortunately, Dan was not ready to apply his new approach in his old world. Nine weeks after he left our program, I received a letter from his mother (see opposite page).

Dan is only one of a number of kids who were not able to sustain their progress after returning home from their wilderness experience. After all, if we look at how long their problem approach was in the making (usually *years!*), it is no wonder that eight weeks cannot completely remedy that. What makes it even harder for these teens to sustain their progress is that they are still vulnerable to the influence of their environments and peer group. It's not that their environments are necessarily negative. Sometimes they just don't support the kinds of changes that these teens need to make. It turns out that things learned in the wilderness are often "use it or lose it" skills.

A Bumpy Road

Dear Paul,

I've missed our weekly calls to speak about Dan. It has been a bumpy road since he left the woods. The first month or so was fine, Dan was polite and willing to talk to me. He would even check in with me whenever he was out, just to let me know where he was. Our therapy sessions were good, and we were considering cutting back to having sessions every other week. Two weeks ago, Dan did not come home on a Thursday night, and didn't call to let me know where he was. I was worried and finally called the police around midnight. They filed a report, but couldn't do much more than issue a missing child alert. At about 3:15 in the morning, I got a call from Dan's girlfriend, who told me that he had taken a "bunch of pills" and was not conscious. I called 911 and rushed to where they were, only to see my unconscious son on a stretcher being placed in the back of an ambulance. Apparently, he had been drinking alcohol with his girlfriend and some of his friends, and they met a guy who had a bunch of OxyContins and Percocets. Dan took a bunch of them and, shortly afterward, appeared to fall asleep. Two hours later, after letting him lie there passed out, his girlfriend tried to wake him up, and couldn't.

When Dan came to in the emergency room, he told me that he had been drinking and doing drugs with his friends for the last couple of weeks. He said he felt so ashamed about it that he couldn't talk to me. A couple of days later, I discovered that Dan has not been going to school regularly, either. I don't know what to do—I feel like we are right back where we were before he went to wilderness.

Transitioning to Therapeutic School

For those coming out of a wilderness program, the transition from wilderness to therapeutic school can be challenging. I usually advise parents not to take their teen home in between enrollments. Most of us who have worked in this field for any time have seen the potential for things to go south quickly. There are valid reasons families want to bring their children home, but it is not recommended. In fact, many schools insist that a child come to campus directly from the wilderness program. As I mentioned earlier, the progress and gains that teens have made during wilderness are still not internalized. They are like new vines that must be held up until they develop the root and stem system necessary to hold themselves up.

For most teens, completion of a wilderness program marks the start of a new kind of relationship with their parents. In many cases, the parents have reestablished their parental authority by sending their child to wilderness or to a therapeutic school. This momentum should not be compromised, even if their child pulls out all the stops to convince them that she is ready to go home. I assure you that it is in the parent's best interest, as well as the child's, to uphold set limits and move forward with getting the teen established in her new environment.

Once parents have dropped off their child at the therapeutic school, I encourage them to join with her treatment team to become a unified group. Concerns or anxieties should always be discussed with the staff team, not with the child. Finally, parents should roll up their sleeves to do the work that they need to do, while trusting the treatment team to provide what is necessary for their child.

Understanding the Therapeutic Process

In order for a child to get what he needs at a therapeutic school or program, it is imperative that his parents be aligned with each other and aligned with the program.[2] Too often, I witness children who cannot get on with their therapeutic work because their parents cannot get on the same page with each other (quite often in situations of divorce). Other times, I see parents actually working against the treatment team and the program structure. Quite often, this is driven by a desire to be seen as "the good parent" in their teen's eyes. In my experience, this is usually a way for parents to relieve their own feelings of guilt about their child. However, if there is a split between the teen's parents or guardians the teens will often play on that split instead of getting on with what he needs to do.

When you enroll your child into a therapeutic school or program, you are joining a team of adults to carry out the tasks of parenting your child through his emotional and behavioral struggles. As problems come up along the way, and they certainly will, your job is to support the treatment team. I am not suggesting that you should not voice questions or concerns, but these should be addressed to the treatment team. The guiding model in therapeutic schools is that of effective parenting. That's why it is so important that parents work with the team of adults in the school to present a unified front for the child.

Although schools and programs differ in their structure, many do limit the student's contact with parents and family initially. Let me explain why I think this is necessary. Once you understand the philosophy, you'll be better prepared to speak to your child's treatment team for a more specific explanation.

There are several things parents should understand about residential therapy. First, residential programs are designed to accomplish therapeutic work through relationships. Therefore, the initial goal is to forge close bonds between the student and her peers, her therapist, and other program staff, so that she becomes integrated and attached to the community. A second reason for the limitations on contact has to do with disrupting over-learned patterns of manipulation and dependency. The goal is to help teens establish new, more effective patterns of relating to others, and program leaders typically want time to understand the dynamics that exist with the teen and his parents, which provides leverage to encourage new ways of interacting. As students progress through the programs, more contact with parents and family members is generally allowed. Visits to the school, opportunities to take the student off campus for weekend visits, additional phone calls home, and, eventually, home visits usually become available as students and families make progress in improving their relationships, in setting or respecting limits, and in communicating more effectively.

Most programs also limit other privileges in the beginning. For example, access to laptops, Internet, iPods and cell phones may be restricted. Communication with friends may also be restricted, as well as opportunities to go off campus into the surrounding community. All of these restrictions limit the teen's opportunities for the teen to act out or to avoid the core therapeutic work. It also provides time for the staff to really get to know the teen and to determine whether he can be trusted to use privileges responsibly. These restrictions also reduce feelings of entitlement and set the stage for helping the teen learn to tolerate frustration and delay gratification. In short, it provides *containment* for the teen's experience, something that many struggling teens desperately need.

A number of therapeutic schools have a "level" system that students are required to move through. The different levels represent milestones in the student's progress and provide a sense of accomplishment as each new level is achieved. Students are often allowed to move through these levels at their own pace, completing various expectations and assignments when they are ready. Obviously, some will climb the ladder faster than others.

Realize that this is part of the process, and remind yourself that accomplishing the objectives of each level is your child's responsibility, not yours.

I also want to say a few words about the rules and structure that each program has in place. Without a doubt, some of these will inconvenience you, and you may well find yourself struggling with your own sense of entitlement in dealing with them. You must understand something here: You are now involved with a village of families who have children in this program. The rules and structure that define what is appropriate and what is not, what is allowed and what is not, and what is expected and what is not tolerated are all necessary to create the kind of cohesive community model that we discussed in chapter one. I really want to stress to you that your approach to the program's rules and structure will impact other parents. In the same way that your teens need to understand how their behavior impacts others, you, too, need to be aware of how your actions affect the community.

Finally, don't miss the forest for the trees! The therapeutic process requires structure in order to succeed, and I assure you that every reputable program is designed with that goal in mind.

Re-entering the Real World

As teens approach the end of their time at a therapeutic school, the focus shifts to the difficult job of determining how to best support their reentry into the "real world." Without a doubt, this is the part of the therapeutic process that schools and programs find most challenging. Many programs offer step-down situations or transition houses, where students remain under the supervision of program leaders as they re-enter mainstream society. Some of these programs house students in community homes, while they take classes at a local community college or school. The students might also hold jobs, allowing them the opportunity to assume the responsibilities of employment and learn how to manage their finances. In these cases, students are gradually given more freedom to integrate into the community, which opens the door for a number of real-world temptations. These include decisions about drugs and alcohol, developing friendships with people not in their program, dating responsibly, and so on.

I also know of programs that provide assistance in students' homes as they transition back into that environment. Initial reports show this might be a useful service for some families, although it may not be widely available. Other programs provide follow-up support to their graduates to help them apply the progress they've made at the school to the real world.

Some students complete their time at a therapeutic school and then transition to a traditional boarding school. Others may go right to college, and some may go home to complete high school in their local community. Whatever the discharge plan, therapeutic programs should offer guidance and advice to students and their parents about realistic options following discharge. Educational consultants continue to be an invaluable resource at this point, as they often have a bead on creative options for making this transition successful.

I generally urge parents in this part of the journey to use caution. Their teens have gained important experience and developed a number of necessary skills during their time at a therapeutic program, and, within a structured and supportive environment, they manage their lives with a degree of maturity they did not have before. However, without an appropriate level of support and structure, these gains continue to be somewhat fragile. It's best to view this transition time as a series of steps, where the student is given opportunities to demonstrate her new approach where the rubber hits the road. One-step-at-a-time transitions also provide an opportunity for parents to practice their new approach for upholding firm and consistent limits with their child.

[1] Levine, M. *The Price of Privilege: How parental pressure and material advantage are creating a generation of disconnected and unhappy kids.* (New York: Harper Collins, 2006).

[2] Baron, Molly. "Therapeutic School Placement: Parallel Process of Change in Children and Their Parents." http://www.natsap.org/pa_thera.asp (2007).

CHAPTER FIVE

HANDING THEM OVER AND HOLDING FAST

What should parents expect from the therapeutic process?

Perhaps some of you have seen the image of the weeping yogi, bent over with his face buried in his hands, moved by the awareness that life is full of both misery and joy, and that one cannot exist without the other. This symbol reminds me of this great truth: No one is exempt from life's misery, that hardship is part of life and is necessary if one is to realize the fullness of being human.

The parenting journey can be full of the highest highs and the lowest lows. Parenting is the ultimate human endeavor. There is no higher calling. The parents I meet, who are in crisis with their teens and desperate to find some way to help them, know well how difficult it is to watch their child struggle. Coming to grips with the fact that they need to send their child away to a therapeutic school or program for a year or more is, for many, a burden beyond description. It strikes at their dreams of how things were supposed to be, and it weighs them down with guilt and sorrow. It is from listening to parents, and trying to ease their burden that I initially became interested in writing this book. My goal is to fill a gap in libraries and in public awareness of just how hard this process can be, and of how alone it makes so many parents feel.

In this chapter, I want to normalize the roller-coaster of emotions that you, as a parent, are likely to experience while your child is away. Feeling these emotions is important, even necessary, so that you can grieve your losses and experience growth and transformation through the process. There will be moments along the way where the desire to pull your child out of a therapeutic program and bring him or her home prematurely may be overwhelming. If I could only give you one piece of advice, it would be this: ***Hold fast, stay the course, and trust the process***. It won't be easy, but I assure you, it's the best thing you can do for your child.

To help you understand what this experience might look and feel like for parents, I am going to organize our discussion around four phases of the therapeutic process. Each phase contains different tasks, emotional experiences, and vulnerabilities for parents as they support and promote the work that their children are doing in the therapeutic program. In each phase, I provide an average timeframe for accomplishment. However, it is important to note that therapeutic programs differ in their lengths and in their treatment approaches, so these timeframes may vary greatly depending on the program and the child. The tables in each section outline the objectives, emotions, vulnerabilities, and tasks that accompany each phase.

Initial Phase: Handing Them Over

The initial phase of getting a child settled in a residential program typically lasts from one to four months, though it does require a bit longer for some families. Often, children and families will first attend a

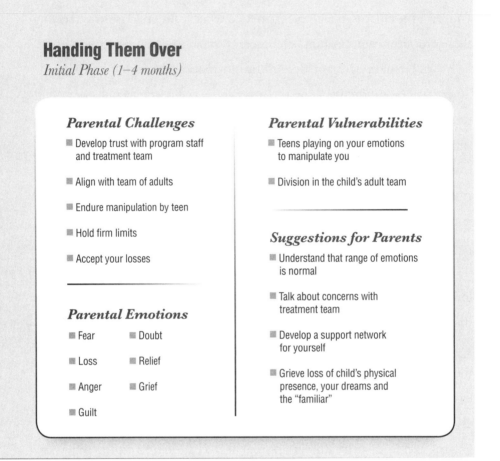

Handing Them Over
Initial Phase (1–4 months)

Parental Challenges

- Develop trust with program staff and treatment team
- Align with team of adults
- Endure manipulation by teen
- Hold firm limits
- Accept your losses

Parental Emotions

- Fear
- Doubt
- Loss
- Relief
- Anger
- Grief
- Guilt

Parental Vulnerabilities

- Teens playing on your emotions to manipulate you
- Division in the child's adult team

Suggestions for Parents

- Understand that range of emotions is normal
- Talk about concerns with treatment team
- Develop a support network for yourself
- Grieve loss of child's physical presence, your dreams and the "familiar"

wilderness program, where they will accomplish much of the work of this phase, making the transition to a therapeutic school much smoother.

The parental tasks you will need to complete during this phase include: developing trust in the treatment team and program structure; aligning yourself with your child's treatment team; and holding a firm limit with your child that communicates your resolve not to waver in your decision to keep her there. This is a time where most parents report feeling raw from the crises that have preceded their decision. They often describe the experience as a whirlwind in which they have had little opportunity to catch their breath and reflect on what has happened. They are following the recommendations of professionals and, at one level, believe that sending their child to a therapeutic program is the right thing to do. However, the act of actually handing their child over into someone else's care can release a floodgate of emotions. In the noticeable calm that exists where there once was crisis, parents quite often suffer an internal storm of fear, doubt, guilt, anger and loss.

All of these feelings are quite normal and are to be expected. Parents fear that they have made the wrong decision, they have doubts about the program, or they worry that their child will not be well cared for. They may worry about their teen's roommates, about whether she is sleeping at night, about how she is eating, and about whether or not she has the right clothes. And they may worry that their child is with other teens who are much sicker and more disturbed.

Many parents also feel a tremendous amount of guilt at this point. They blame themselves for their child's problems, and may feel that they should probably be the ones in treatment. Many harbor a desire to undo their past mistakes. This leads to ambivalence about the choice they have made, and they may harbor fantasies that, with appropriate willpower and changes on their end, they could make it work with their child at home.

And then there are the feelings of loss. None of the parents I've met ever dreamt that someday they would send their child to a residential therapeutic program. And they see the dreams they did have turn to dust: dreams of taking pictures of their daughter before her junior prom; dreams of watching their son play on the varsity lacrosse team; or dreams of being together at the annual family reunion in Lake Tahoe. What's more, they miss their child's physical presence, and the empty chair at the dinner table is a constant reminder of their loss. One mother described to me how she felt after her daughter enrolled in a therapeutic program. Every night she would go into her daughter's room, sit on the bed and cry as she looked at all of the pictures tacked on the bedroom door, each of them reminding her of when her daughter was still a happy girl.

Some days are better than others, parents say. But some days feel downright unbearable. And they are angry about how difficult it is to solve this problem with their teen. Angry that it requires something like wilderness or a therapeutic school. Angry that other families are not having to endure this loss. Angry that the program has so many damned restrictions! Angry that they feel so alone.

And then there are those who feel relieved. Relieved that their child is somewhere safe and is getting the help he or she needs. Relieved that they do not have to worry about where their child is tonight, or when the inevitable yelling match will start. Relieved that they can invest time and energy in their marriage, or their other children, or their own self-development. And, in vulnerable moments, these parents often feel guilty for feeling relieved.

All of these feelings are normal. I encourage parents to talk about these feelings with their child's treatment team, because it is important

"Rescue Me!"

My colleagues and I often tell parents that they should prepare themselves to receive one of three types of letters from their kids after they arrive at a program.

One is the "screw you" letter, which basically tells parents, "This is the most ridiculous decision any parent could ever make and, if you do not get me out of here, you can kiss our relationship goodbye!"

Another is the "miracle cure" letter. It says, "Dear Mom and Dad, I get it. I want a good relationship with you. I never want it to be like it was, and I will never do any of the things I was doing before. I just want to be at home and have a happy family."

And then there is the "truth about this place" letter: "This place is awful. All the kids are drug addicts and a lot of them have been in jail. They don't feed us enough, and the food sucks! And I don't get to put the time into my homework that I need to in order to get into a good college!"

during these times that they trust and feel committed to the process. I also encourage parents to find other sources of support, to reach out to friends, family members, pastors, or therapists. Parents are grieving at this point, and they need to talk about their feelings and receive support.

Beware of Manipulative Tactics

The goal for parents, of course, is to endure these feelings and hold the line. Teens *will* go after any parental vulnerability. It has worked for them before, and it is a well-developed tactic among teens. Pushing parental buttons and playing on their fears or feelings of guilt is what teens do when they are anxious, uncomfortable, or faced with limits and consequences they do not like.

Other teens will attempt to manipulate parents and school staff by refusing to communicate, by withdrawing, or by not engaging in the program. Sometimes they will threaten to hurt themselves. Often they will drag up every mistake and every cross word a parent has ever uttered, blaming their parents for every poor decision they themselves have made. Whatever the tactic, the goal is always the same: They want to be

REAL TIME

Impact Letter

Dear Chris:

There are many reasons your mother and I decided to send you to the wilderness. Your poor frustration tolerance and anger control is a major problem. Smashing a hole in the front of your bedroom door in response to mom not letting you take her CD player to school last week was the most recent destruction of property. The back of your bedroom door, the front of your closet door, the garage door, and the laundry room were all damaged by your previous bursts of anger.

These events affected me in several ways. I am very hurt that you do not respect our property more. A nice, comfortable, and safe house is not easy to obtain and maintain. I have heard your mother say "we can't have nice things around here." It upsets me a great deal to see you take our property for granted. It shows disrespect for your mother and I. I also feel sad for you, because I know that you must be unhappy with yourself and in pain.

Marijuana use is another reason you were removed from our home. I have never actually caught you smoking marijuana. Your mom and I have found it in your room. We have recovered bongs, tweezers, clips, bags with seeds, and other items from your room. I found a bong outside your bedroom window a few weeks ago while doing yardwork. Your mom found two small marijuana plants in your closet. When the policeman was in your room after you destroyed your bedroom door last week, you had marijuana seeds on your desk. What puzzles me is that you knew the police officer was coming, and you still did not seem to care.

These actions anger and scare me. Continually having illegal substances in our home despite being told that it won't be tolerated shows total lack of respect to your mom and I and for the law. I am afraid for you because I do not think you realize how close you are to being arrested and having lifelong consequences. In my opinion, your actions indicate a need for help and immediate intervention.

You needed to be removed from your present school. Though you were making progress towards high school graduation until this semester, you have now reached a point where you do no homework and are failing all four of your classes. You often skip classes. You won't let anyone help you with your schoolwork. I know that you have learning disabilities, but your unwillingness to receive help is putting your future at risk.

I have been hiding my wallet for the past few months. You often tell us you owe people money for gas or food. Several times, your mom and I have both discovered money missing from our wallets, and we are pretty sure that you have been taking it. It has caused us both to not be able to trust you, or to feel safe sharing a home with you.

You have used vulgar language around the house. You use the "F" word a lot. Two weeks ago you called your mother "a fucking whore" in a fit of anger. After you calmed down, I told you that was totally unacceptable. You had no response. Your little sister often hears you saying vulgar things, and you do not seem to care.

The bad language and other problems listed above have made our home a poor environment to live in and to raise your sister. I love you and your sister both very much, but I felt it was necessary to temporarily remove you from the home so that you could get help. I believe the wilderness program can help you in many ways. You used to be a happy boy, and I believe they can help you develop your self-esteem and find more inner happiness. You need someone other than your parents to help you understand how destructive your current behavior is. You either won't listen to us, or you do not respect us enough to listen to what we say. I hope you can develop more confidence in yourself and learn to focus more on the positive things in your life.

You have many good qualities. You are an attractive young man. I remember walking out of IHOP a few weeks ago and a young female hostess was smiling at you and telling you to never cut your hair. When you are happy, you have charm and charisma. You are a good athlete. I remember actually crying for joy after you ran out a home run to win a baseball game a couple of years ago. I was thrilled to see you so happy. I have loved watching you play on your high school lacrosse team, and seeing how excited you get when the team plays well.

You recently started working with a lawn service on Saturdays. You worked hard, and your boss told me that you were a role model to his 12-year-old son. That made me proud and happy. You can and will work hard if you know what needs to be done and can see the benefit. I hope your time in the wilderness can help you find a direction for your life that you can pursue and feel good about.

You love and care for your little sister. She cried the day that you left for the wilderness, and she put a large picture of you by her bed. We will all miss you while you are away, but we want you to take a good look at your life and think about the decisions you are making. I will always love you, and look forward to seeing you when you are ready.

Love,
Dad

rescued from their frustration, and they want to avoid the hard work of completing the program and growing up!

It is critical that you understand that your resolve and your unwillingness to give in to manipulation is actually what will allow your teen to move beyond these immature ways of dealing with distress. In the midst of all of the emotions that you are feeling, your insistence that you will not go back to the way things were and that you will not negotiate is the best thing that you can do for your child and for your relationship. It is the kind of experience they need.

I encourage parents during this initial phase of treatment to put in writing all the concerns they have about their child's behavior and attitude. A number of programs ask parents to write a letter to their child in the first couple of weeks that clearly and specifically states why they made the decision to send the teen to a therapeutic program or school. (See Impact Letter on page 108.) As parents go through the various emotions of the early months, I encourage them to review regularly the reasons they sent their child away. Keep them fresh in your mind!

I also ask parents to consider this question: *What kind of adult do you want your child to become?* Your answer is your goal. In order for your child to become the adult you hope for, he will require certain experiences that he will receive in his new therapeutic environments. For example, he will experience what it's like to be known by and connected to a community of adults and peers, who share similar expectations and behavioral norms. He will also experience being held accountable for his choices and will face natural consequences, both positive and negative, of his actions.

Dealing with Ambivalence

Let me say a word about parental ambivalence. It is probably the biggest barrier to getting teens to accept their new situation, to accept the new limits their parents have set, and to work through their own process of grief. Ambivalence is not always communicated directly to teens. However, teens can often sense when their parents are having mixed feelings about a program, or are having doubts about sending their teen away, or are wavering in their support of the treatment team. So, I urge parents to resolve their own ambivalence about this decision. Often, it is connected to their own grief process. The child's treatment team and educational consultant can be resources, as can a parent's own therapist.

I believe the resolution of ambivalence comes about when parents accept that their child needed this intervention to develop a more mature approach to his life. Uncertainties about this kind of intervention may be driven by fantasies that things would have gotten better in time, or by worries that this situation may do irreparable damage to the parent-child relationship. The reality, though, is that without certain therapeutic experiences, these teens may never develop a mature approach to life. And because so many of the teens enrolled in therapeutic programs are unable to make changes using outpatient resources, they are often facing potentially devastating consequences if they cannot control their behavior. Once parents see this decision as a way of giving their child the experiences they need, it's easier to accept the hard parts of this challenge and to keep moving forward.

As for parents' worries about further damaging their relationship with their teen, in reality that relationship is already under pressure that will not be relieved until entrenched patterns of manipulation by the teen and unresolved tension and resentments between parent and child are addressed. Fortunately, the relationship between parents and their teen is the focus of much of the therapeutic work in residential programs and, more often that not, improvements can be realized. Better yet, because the treatment team and program staff often assume the parental role of setting limits and enforcing boundaries for the teen, parents get a respite from power struggles. This opens the door for parents to begin rebuilding and repairing the relationship with their son or daughter.

Let me quickly address another practical issue that comes up during this initial phase of the therapeutic process. Parents often ask me what they should tell siblings, relatives, or friends about their child being in a therapeutic program. There is not one hard and fast rule about this. In many ways, it depends on the child's feelings and family's comfort level with speaking about these circumstances. I will say that you have no obligation to disclose anything. Quite often, simply letting people know that your child is at boarding school is enough.

With siblings and relatives, however, it may be necessary to disclose more details about why the teen is away. Because there are so many variables at play—the circumstances surrounding the decision, the age of siblings and their relationship with the teen, the relationship teens have with relatives, and your family members' tendencies to be either judgmental or supportive —it is best to speak with your child's therapist about how to address your specific situation. Assuring your family that your child is in a safe place, where he or she is getting the help they need, can go a long way in alleviating their anxieties and worries.

Parental Ambivalence

Mark and Jeri were having a very hard time with their daughter, Liz, who they had recently sent to a therapeutic school. Week after week, during parent phone calls, Liz would complain about how she wanted to be home, how she didn't really like any of her peers at the school, how she wasn't making any progress on getting her checklist signed off so that she could move forward in the program. And week after week, Mark and Jeri would respond with lame comments about how Liz might feel better if she would try to engage in the program. Then, after Liz got off the phone, they would moan and complain to me about whether or not this was really the right thing to do. They particularly felt bad because Liz was adopted, and they did not want her to feel abandoned.

I was sympathetic to their anxiety for several weeks. Then I began to realize that their ambivalence about their decision was actually preventing Liz from fully engaging in the community like she needed to. In fact, I explained to Mark and Jeri that Liz was taking her cue from them, and that she would continue to resist engagement until they convinced her that they were committed to her working the program. I assured them that I had seen this dynamic a number of times, and asked them to remember the circumstances that prompted them to send Liz to the school in the first place. As we reviewed their decision, they came to realize that, although they wanted Liz home, they knew she would not be able to make the improvements there that she needed. They knew that she would get caught up again with her negative peer group, that she would refuse school, and that she would probably once again become very sneaky with drugs and sexual acting out.

Mark and Jeri mustered their resolve and wrote Liz a letter explaining that coming home at this time was not an option, that they believed they had made a smart decision in choosing a therapeutic school for her, and that they expected her to get on with doing what she needed to do to move through the program. On our weekly phone calls, Mark and Jeri began to have a different tone with Liz, and though Liz initially responded with more complaints, she eventually got the message. Liz began to work the program and to connect with her community, making friends with peers and with staff. Soon, the weekly phone calls were no longer filled with complaints, but with Liz reporting to her parents about what she was doing in the program, and who she was connecting with.

Middle Phase: Working the Program

The middle phase of the therapeutic process typically lasts from four to eight months (depending on the program) and begins after parents have weathered the storms of handing the kids over, making their own emotional adjustments, and enduring the teen's testing and manipulation. Once these storms subside, and teens realize that their parents are not going to bend, they usually will settle down and get to work on their therapeutic objectives. This is a welcome experience for most parents, who finally begin to feel that this intervention is helping, that this is the right place for their child, and that there is hope. The teen settles into a routine as the parents become more familiar with the program structure and the professionals working with their child. Parents also are getting used to the fact of their child being away, though they may never find it easy.

During this phase, your task as a parent is to remain firmly resolved that your child will complete his therapeutic program. You also want to recognize improvements in your child's attitude and behavior, to focus on implementing the new strategies and skills that you and your child are developing, and to engage in marital and family work needed to support the changes your child is making.

Don't be surprised if family dynamics undergo major shifts during this period. Without even knowing it, your family has organized itself around your problem child. He has often been the source of anxiety and conflict, and he's taxed everybody's resources. Each member has adapted ways to cope with this stress and has internalized unspoken rules about how to deal with the anxiety in your home. These might include rules about what is okay and not okay to talk about, or about how to avoid

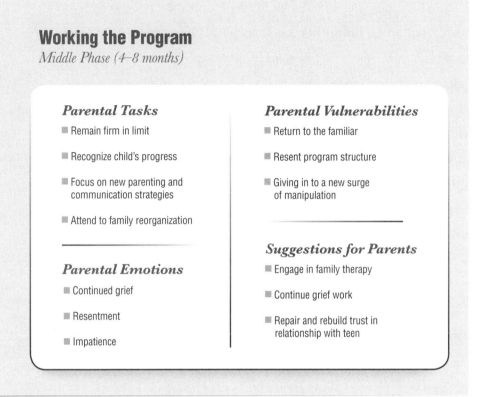

Working the Program
Middle Phase (4–8 months)

Parental Tasks

- Remain firm in limit

- Recognize child's progress

- Focus on new parenting and communication strategies

- Attend to family reorganization

Parental Emotions

- Continued grief

- Resentment

- Impatience

Parental Vulnerabilities

- Return to the familiar

- Resent program structure

- Giving in to a new surge of manipulation

Suggestions for Parents

- Engage in family therapy

- Continue grief work

- Repair and rebuild trust in relationship with teen

certain conflicts. Family members have established patterns that govern how they take care of each other, who they rely on to be strong, and what they do to gain attention or feel close to each other.

Once a problem child is out of the house, it becomes apparent that he was playing a very important role in the family. Because he consumed so much attention, family issues were neglected that now need to be addressed. This is the work of family therapy, and I strongly encourage you to engage in this process in order to reorganize your family to function in a healthy way. Otherwise, you are vulnerable to returning to familiar and often dysfunctional patterns.

I've seen some parents pull their child out of a therapeutic program during this phase because the family reorganization process feels too unfamiliar and is producing much anxiety: *Now what do we do? Now what do we talk about? Now what?* Instead of addressing the issues that are making them feel uncomfortable, such as marital dissatisfaction, parents succumb to the temptation to restore the old balance by bringing the child home. Their unspoken expectation is that this child will once again absorb the family's anxiety. The sad thing is that, while they are soothing their own discomfort, these parents are relinquishing their responsibility to provide their child with the kinds of experiences he needs to develop and mature.

Struggling with Resentment

Another vulnerability parents face in the middle phase of treatment, especially once they begin to see positive changes in their child, is resentment of the process. This can be hard for parents to admit because they are also very pleased about their child's progress. But, I've heard from a number of parents over the years that they resent not being able to experience their child's progress and improvement on a daily basis.

"I wish we could have had more time like this when she was home," one mother complained. "Why can't she come home now, since she is doing so much better? We don't have much time left for her to live at home – does the program really have to be so long?"

Parents also may feel resentment about the financial strain this process causes. Although parents are often willing to provide whatever is needed for their children, there is no denying that therapeutic schools and programs can be very costly. I believe it is valid for parents to resent the length and cost of the process from time to time. It is important that these parents feel comfortable talking about it, so that these concerns do not undermine their commitment to the program.

Many parents find it difficult to maintain their resolve during this period. They may struggle to adhere to program requirements and expectations. Parental visits, for example, which are often short and somewhat structured, become an opportunity for parents to ignore rules or loosen boundaries. Some of it is driven by a desire to win their child's favor. Some of it is probably just a remnant of the old way of doing business. But, whatever the reason, it is so important that parents talk about this with their child's treatment team or their own therapist. It is wonderful to see a child's progress, but it is important to remember that internalizing these gains takes time.

It is also important to understand the continued role that you as a parent must play, which is to maintain limits and expectations firmly and consistently. Although you have relinquished much of the day-in and day-out responsibility for your teen, your commitment to this process enables school staff to do the needed work with your teen that will create lasting change. In addition, you are modeling for your child a commitment to finish what they've started, even when the process becomes frustrating or challenging.

Discharge Phase: Keeping it Real

If you are just beginning the process of getting your child therapeutic treatment in a residential program, it may be hard to imagine that it will reach an end, but it will. Hopefully, by that point, you and your teen will have grown in some very important ways, and you will see evidence that she has matured in her decision-making. If all has gone as planned, you also will have restored your parental authority and become more accurately attuned to your teen, validating her developmental progress, while maintaining firm limits as to what you will and will not tolerate.

The tasks for parents during the discharge phase include working with their teens to create a thoughtful and realistic plan for what's next. The reality is that these teens will be transitioning from a structured environment that supports and promotes mature behavior into one that will likely have less structure and less built-in support. Do not underestimate how challenging it is for teens to be thrust into a less supportive environment, even if they have functioned very well in the therapeutic school. Be careful not to slip back into the mentality of the medical model approach that says "we've treated the problem and it's cured!" The cure, if there is one, is that your teen has developed the ability to make better decisions, and you as parents have developed the ability to provide accurate attunement and containment. This new *process* is what has been established. Now, it will need to be implemented.

Parents should consult with their child's therapist or program advisor to determine whether the transition should be back home or to a step-down environment. As I mentioned in the previous chapter, there are op-

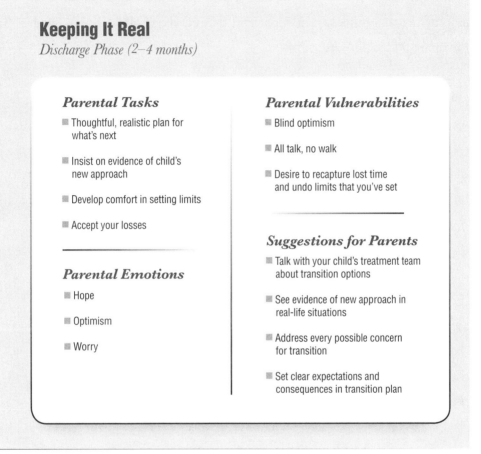

Keeping It Real
Discharge Phase (2–4 months)

Parental Tasks

- Thoughtful, realistic plan for what's next

- Insist on evidence of child's new approach

- Develop comfort in setting limits

- Accept your losses

Parental Emotions

- Hope

- Optimism

- Worry

Parental Vulnerabilities

- Blind optimism

- All talk, no walk

- Desire to recapture lost time and undo limits that you've set

Suggestions for Parents

- Talk with your child's treatment team about transition options

- See evidence of new approach in real-life situations

- Address every possible concern for transition

- Set clear expectations and consequences in transition plan

tions for helping teens transition back to "real-world" environments, and it's best to get professional guidance about what your teen may need.

Most programs help students and their families create a relapse prevention plan or discharge plan. In my experience, this is an excellent opportunity for parents to solidify their re-established authority with the teen. Let me suggest something to you boldly: *Do not tolerate a mediocre job with this!* This exercise must realistically consider what transitioning out of the structured milieu might entail. The temptation will be strong to employ magical thinking and gloss over the real-life challenges that await the teen and his parents.

I believe that parents need to be very clear about what they will and will not tolerate, as well as about what the consequences will be if the teen makes certain decisions. Work with your child's treatment team to make this more than just a last-minute assignment that the child dashes off in order to finish the program. Also, approach this process with the mindset that this is an agreement between you and your teen. In my experience, contracts that merely demand certain things from teens often do not work very well. I believe it is important that parents clearly spell out their expectations for their teens and list the parental response for failure to meet expectations. Parents must come to an agreement on the follow-through here. That way, when a breach of the expectations occurs, the consequence will not be up for discussion or debate, and the possibility for manipulation is blocked.

Another important parental task prior to discharge is to insist that your son or daughter provide evidence of his or her new approach. Most programs integrate opportunities for teens to manage higher levels of freedom. These typically include visits home, where they must follow their parent's guidelines and requests. They may also be allowed to interact again with old peers or acquaintances. Before you assume that your teen has completed his or her work at a therapeutic school, you must see that demonstrated in environments that are not highly structured.

Parents are very vulnerable at this point to blind optimism. They are so hopeful that their teens have "gotten it," and so amazed at their ability to say the right things, that they put trust in the talk, without seeing the walk. For some, there is an underlying desire to "undo" lost time with their child, particularly the times of conflict and struggle. They may, therefore, forget the need for structure and firm expectations. They want so much to believe that all is going to be well for their teen, and it can be. But, it can also be a time of great disappointment and shame if parents do not approach this transition with a measure of caution.

Transition Phase: Letting the Reins Out Slowly

Once teens graduate from their therapeutic school or program, they begin their transition back into the real world. They are now back under the supervision of their parents, and although this phase usually begins with a celebration for completing the program, it also launches a new period of readjusting to real life back home. The goal for parents is to let the reins out slowly. Even though your teenager has done important work during his or her therapeutic program, they are still teenagers and need their parents to remember that.

The major parental tasks of this phase are to follow and revise the relapse-prevention plan or discharge plan that was developed prior to leaving the therapeutic school or program. I recommend that parents meet weekly with their teenager to review progress on the transition plan and to make revisions as needed. The expectations of the plan should be loosened very cautiously. I recommend that no loosening of plan boundaries occur until the teen has maintained himself and met expectations for at least two to three months. Parents should expect there to be a "honeymoon period," when things go very well. However, remember that one of the changes that parents have hopefully made during the time their child has been away is to develop more comfort and authority in setting and maintaining prudent limits.

Keep this in mind: Most of you are essentially going through a process designed to teach your teenager about trust. Rebuilding trust once it is broken can be a long, slow process that requires consistency. This is your opportunity, and it is your parental obligation, to facilitate the restoration of trust and to demonstrate how essential it is within relationships. In fact, trust is the foundation of relationships, and your teen will need to understand that if he or she is to build healthy intimate relationships with others.

Staying connected

Another major parental task is to maintain connection with their teen. This will require time and intention on both sides. One suggestion is that the family commit to "unplugged" family time, where iPods are put away, cell phones are set aside, and the Internet and video games are turned off. Regular family meals together can provide this time. Interestingly, this is one of the "structures" of the family that many of us grew up with and expected. Today's teens, in contrast, rarely spend time with their parents uninterrupted by one of the multitude of distractions our culture offers. Because your teen will have had plenty of opportunity to be unplugged from distractions during their therapeutic program, it should not seem like an unreasonable request to continue this practice at home.

Letting the Reins Out Slowly

Transition Phase (3–12 months)

Parental Tasks

- Follow discharge plan
- Continue to uphold limits
- Maintain connection and relationship

Suggestions for Parents

- Set aside regular "unplugged" time
- Insist on reciprocity in relationships
- Give choices and then allow consequences
- Follow through consistently
- Revisit discharge plan regularly

Parental Vulnerabilities

- Allow too much, too soon
- Let "small" slips slide
- Buy into teen's entitlement feelings
- Micro-manage in a way that removes teen's choices
- Return to old patterns

Parental Emotions

- Optimism
- Confidence
- Discouragement
- Worry

Spend time with your teen's peer group, as well. Remember, the influence of peers is tremendously powerful during adolescence, and the influence of negative peers can truly sabotage many of the gains that your teenager has made. Give your teen choices as they reintegrate with peers, so that they have an opportunity to demonstrate that they can manage things well, while knowing what the consequences will be should they make poor decisions. You must be prepared to follow through with consequences so that they do not become seen as empty threats.

In Transition

Not long ago, I received a call from the mother of a boy that I had counseled several years ago. She called to tell me the good news that he was completing his senior year of high school at home, and he had just been accepted into a prestigious college. When I asked her about the transition experience, she admitted that it had been difficult at times. She attributed their ability to make it through the hard times to their work with a family therapist. She reported that he normalized their experience, and supported them all as they put into practice the things they had learned while her son was attending therapeutic school. And, she said, he kept them from becoming too discouraged or anxious.

In addition, insist that your teen's decisions take into account and demonstrate concern for how they will affect their relationship with you. By holding your teen to this standard, you teach them to value their relationships and think about how their decisions impact others. Of course, you should reciprocate by considering what impact your decisions will have on your child.

Another task of the transition phase is for parents and teens to utilize professional support within their community. This can be a family therapist, a psychiatrist, or some other professional who understands the transition process and can provide support for the family.

During the transition phase, many parents feel a mixture of confidence and optimism, along with an inclination to worry. There is a desire to avoid the mistakes of the past, and when behaviors or interactions trigger recollections of the way things used to be, it can create a high level of anxiety. When this happens, I urge parents to remind themselves that they have developed a new way of dealing with their teen. It is so important, especially during the transition time, that parents approach bumps in the road, even minor relapses, as opportunities to put into practice their new parental responses. They must be persistent in applying limits and expect their teen to demonstrate respect for their relationship by complying with their rules.

It is not uncommon for teens, once they get out of a therapeutic program, to experience a relapse of old patterns or behaviors. Sometimes these relapses can actually be quite serious and can leave parents feeling tremendously discouraged. According to researchers who have studied the way that people change problematic behaviors, relapse tends to be part of the process.[1] What I have seen, and what many of my colleagues report, is that teens typically step down from the structure of the therapeutic school or program, and, after a honeymoon period, fall on their face. What is interesting, however, is that they usually pick themselves up and demonstrate an internal motivation to continue moving ahead with their progress. This appears to be especially true if their parents are available to them, are able to manage their own emotions about the relapse without assuming it's a catastrophe, and continue to uphold clear expectations and limits. Perhaps this ability to pick themselves up after a relapse is an indicator that these teens have, in fact, developed a more mature approach to life through their experiences at a therapeutic school.

Parents are vulnerable to a number of temptations during this phase of the process. The first is that they want to let the reins out too quickly by not providing enough structure for the teen. It is easy to underestimate the fragility of their children's gains at this point. Often parents begin to let small things slide, which conveys to the teen that their limits are not really meant to be followed. Furthermore, parents are vulnerable to being manipulated by teens, who use the fact that they have been away so long at a therapeutic program to convince parents that they deserve to be given "normal" freedoms. Holding the line in these moments is so important, even though it may feel very uncomfortable for parents and teens. One might say that it is the teen's job to test the parents' limits, but it is certainly the parents' job to uphold them and enforce them consistently.

Another area of vulnerability for parents is their inclination to micromanage their teen's behavior. Teens must have freedom to choose if they are to practice their new life skills. I always suggest that parents provide options for the teen and spell out the consequences for not meeting expectations. Remember, you cannot make a teen choose what you want, but you can limit the options, and then allow the teen's choice to be met with the appropriate consequences, good and bad. Of course, you must be willing to follow through with those consequences. I'll discuss this process more in chapter six.

Now that you have a better idea of what to expect when your child is involved with a therapeutic program or school, I'd like to introduce you to the therapeutic work that you need to do while your teen is away. In chapter six, you will learn more about how you can grow and develop your parenting abilities so that you will be better able to support and sustain the gains that your teen is making at his or her therapeutic school or program.

---

[1] Prochaska, J.O. and C.C. DiClemente. "Stages and processes of self-change of smoking: Toward an integrative model of change." *Journal of Consulting and Clinical Psychology*, no. 51 (1983): 390-395.

CHAPTER SIX

DOING YOUR WORK

Are you ready and willing to grow as a parent?

Recently, while speaking with the father of a young man that was under my care at a wilderness program, the father told me, in a voice shaking with emotion, that he worries that his son's problems are the result of his poor job of parenting. Have you ever wondered the same thing? Most parents do.

In fact, it's quite common for parents to ask me what they should be working on while their child is away at a therapeutic school or program. I am always happy to hear this question because teens' problems don't arise in a vacuum, and I believe parents must make changes in their parenting style if they want their struggling teen to succeed in maintaining his or her own changes. However, before I offer any advice about what you can work on while your son or daughter is away at a therapeutic program or school, I want to be very clear about a couple of things.

First, it is a very difficult age in which to parent. Numerous factors in our contemporary culture make it extremely challenging for parents to raise children into adults. Not only do incessant distractions pull at you and your kids, but the lack of shared community values about parenting means you likely receive little or no support. And these are but a couple of the obstacles that parents must face today.

Second, and I won't sugar-coat this, your parenting does play a part in your teen's struggles and difficulties. Of course it does. That does not mean you are to blame for all your child's difficulties. However, there are certainly things that you can do to improve your relationship with your teen and help him navigate the rocky road ahead. As we look at the changes you may need to make, I urge you to be kind to yourself. This is not a time for excessive guilt or anxiety at your parental shortcomings. Instead, I suggest that you view the time that your teen is away at a therapeutic program as an opportunity to invest in your own growth and development. I strongly encourage you to engage in your own therapeutic process, to explore your experiences as a parent, and to evaluate your overall approach to parenting.

One of the most important principles of effective parenting is flexibility. You must be willing to adjust your parenting approach based on the needs of your child or teen. This is what makes attunement to your child possible. If you're like most parents, you are doing the very best you can to parent your struggling teen. Yet, your approach may not be adequate for that particular child or for that child's stage of development or specific circumstances. What I'm alluding to here is what developmental psychologists call the "fit" between parent and child. In a good parent-child fit, the parent's manner of caregiving blends well with the child's temperament. However, in a poor fit, the parent's style does not mesh well with the way the child receives care or expresses needs. Over time, poor fit breeds resentment, exhaustion, and conflict due to the inability of the parents and child to get into sync with each other. After all, parenting is not something that you do *to* a child, but something you do *with* a child. And we all understand that children are not blank slates when they arrive into this world. Instead, they come pre-wired with their own energy level, waking and eating cycles, capacity to be soothed, and intensity of reactions to discomfort.

How many of you have joked at one time or another that it's too bad children do not come with owner's manuals? Imagine a how-to book that could provide the right parental response for every situation. It would tell you what to do when the child does this or that, or better yet, what you should *not* say or do when your child does *that*. To be sure, there are good parenting books that offer wise strategies on how to deal with children during their first year, their school years, and even their adolescent years. And, many of you may be so familiar with a particular book that you can quote entire sections from it. But, the frustration I continually hear from parents is that these books "don't really describe *my* child," or that the strategies sound great, but "they don't work on Jimmy."

Unfortunately, no one can provide you with a parenting manual for your particular struggling teen. Certainly, your child's treatment team at the program where he or she is enrolled can offer specific strategies to help you help your child, but ultimately you must do the work. That is why, in this chapter, I want to turn the spotlight on you and ask you to examine how this particular child is affecting you. I am not looking for a list of complaints about your child's behavior. Rather, I want you to begin thinking about your role in the difficulties your teen is having. Have you considered that your struggling teen may feel frustrated that his or her strategy for moving from childhood to adulthood is not acceptable to you? I ask this not to lay blame, but to point out that many problems that arise in the process of parenting ultimately spring from a poor fit between parent and child. In other words, what this particular child wants or requires at this juncture in her development may conflict with what you are able or willing to provide.

A poor fit between you and your child can be attributed to many causes. You may have too many demands on your time and energy to provide the *relationship experiences* that your child needs to develop a more mature approach to his life. Perhaps you believe that, no matter what you sacrifice or do for your child, he'll never respond in the way you wish he would. Perhaps your son or daughter makes you feel like a failure as a parent, and you have lost hope that you can ever do the right thing.

That's how many of the parents with whom I work are feeling when we first meet. They have decided to take the drastic step of sending their child *somewhere* so that *someone* can do the right thing to help their struggling teen. Fortunately, I can reassure them that sending their child away to a reputable therapeutic school or program can help, but with one caveat. In my experience, parents must also do their own transformational work while their child is away. By doing so, parents significantly increase the odds that their teen will not only make improvements while away, but will be able to maintain those improvements over time. And this appears to be supported by studies of outcomes for children and adolescents after residential care.[1]

So what might *your* transformational work be? First, I want you to consider your own level of maturity, as evidenced by how you approach the tasks and demands that face you, as well as how you parent your child.

Different Strokes

If you have more than one child in your family, you've seen how a parenting approach that works well for one child may not work for others. And you don't really know why. Jay and Lisa described to me how they did everything the same in parenting their older daughter and their younger daughter, Chalise, who they were enrolling in a therapeutic program.

"Our older daughter never gave us any problems. She struggled with us at times over schoolwork, but she always got it done. She went out with her friends in high school, she drank some, got into a little bit of trouble, but she always made good grades, and when we put our foot down, she respected us.

"Chalise, on the other hand, has always struggled over schoolwork, but she never gets it done without one of us having to stand over her and watch her do it. When we put our foot down with her, or should we say, when we stomp our foot in a tantrum, she just continues to do whatever she wants, seemingly oblivious to our frustration."

Second, I encourage you to reflect on your parenting style, especially when it comes to attunement with your child's needs and setting appropriate limits for your child. Third, I challenge you to address family patterns that may be negatively impacting your teen in his or her development. And, finally, I want to introduce the idea that you need a coherent narrative about your own life experiences if you hope to develop a healthy relationship with your child.

Your Own Level of Maturity

You may laugh when I ask you where you are in terms of maturity. However, just because you are an adult and face adult challenges day in and day out does not automatically mean that you approach your life with maturity. In fact, when you read the dimensions of the immature approach in chapter two, you may have recognized behavioral traits of adult friends, colleagues, bosses, and even yourself. This does not mean, of course, that all those adults are pathologically immature. Most of us occasionally act or approach decisions in an immature manner. For example, who has not made a decision that could be considered impulsive and without regard for future consequences? And who among us can say we have never treated other people as if they existed only to satisfy our needs and wants? What about that waiter at the restaurant, who seemed to be ignoring your table when you were in a hurry?

None of us is perfect. What I am concerned about are the more enduring qualities you display in your approach to life. Perhaps you characteristically respond to certain situations in ways that indicate a chronic sense of entitlement. Or you treat others, even those closest to you, with a lack of empathy. Or you portray an attitude to your children that indicates you believe certain rules do not apply to you, that you can break them whenever you like, or whenever there is an obvious reward with no clear threat of punishment. Or you use rigid black-and-white thinking to determine what is the right way to think or feel or act in certain situations, leaving no room for someone (like your child) to have a different point of view.

As your adolescent struggles to grow up and develop a working approach to relationships, self-regulation, and goal-oriented behavior, he or she may challenge you to examine how you approach the demands of your life. Believe me, your teen knows your general way of doing business, whether or not they understand it as mature or immature. And, if you are urging them to develop a new approach to their world and their relationships that is inconsistent with your own approach, they will likely resist or engage you in a power struggle until you demonstrate important changes in your own way of doing business. Adolescents pay more attention to what they observe than to what they hear. Any parent who has attempted to use logic to persuade their teen to change can attest to that!

Relationships and Parental Narcissism

Perhaps the most common problem I see in parents is a tendency towards narcissistic or dependent relationships, particularly in their parenting. Parental narcissism prevents parents from being attuned to their child's needs, wants, and developing sense of self. Narcissism causes us to see ourselves when we look at others. We may look at our children and see in them the things we do or do not like about ourselves, and then reflect back to them that they should be different than they are. Narcissistic parents treat their children as if they are extensions of themselves, not as separate beings with their own evolving personalities. Narcissistic parents have agendas for their children, and often there is an unspoken threat to the child if she does not fulfill those agendas. These threats may include abandonment, withdrawal of love and acceptance, or shame-based messages given to the child when they express their unique individuality.

Levine writes:

[P]arents' demands for achievement have all but crowded out kids' internal push toward autonomy. It is hard to develop an authentic sense of self when there is constant pressure to adopt a socially facile, highly competitive, performance-oriented, unblemished self that is promoted by omnipresent adults. This may encourage some children to perform at high levels, but, more important, it also encourages dependency, depression, and a truncated sense of self in most children.[2]

This is the fallout when parents' agendas are allowed to override the interests of their children.

Narcissistic parents treat their children as if they exist to meet the needs of the parent. This inevitably interferes with the child's needs to venture out from the dependency that characterized the early parent-child relationship. Children need to explore the world, and they need to do so while seeing a healthy reflection of self in the mirror of their parents' responses. Parental responsiveness will, of course, sometimes come with limits to the child's explorations. In healthy parenting, the limit will be applied to keep the child safe, and it will reflect an accurate awareness of the child's developmental level. Narcissistic parental limits, on the other hand, will be guided by the parent's needs, wants, or anxieties, which provides an altogether different motive that potentially disregards what is best for the child. And, quite often, narcissistic-driven limits are set in a flare of emotion that may communicate shame, disgust, and harshness towards the teen.

Children of narcissistic parents often have trouble recognizing their own feelings or opinions. They may constantly be looking to others for some sort of indication as to how they should behave, or how they should think and feel. They may lack any clear sense of a stable identity. Instead, they will take whatever role needs to be filled in a particular situation. These children may be desperate for some validation from others, and may be willing to go to great lengths to attract attention or approval. Or, they may become angry when demands are placed upon them, resentful that their wants and needs have constantly been rejected or belittled by their parents, and determined to go their own way without regard for what anyone else thinks or feels.

Please understand that I am not suggesting that all narcissistic parents would qualify for a diagnosis of narcissistic personality disorder. Narcissistic parenting is a parenting approach, and you do not have to be a *bona fide* narcissist to carry it out. Narcissistic parenting is a failure in attunement to the valid needs, feelings, and beliefs of your child that springs from a preoccupation with the parent's own needs, feelings and beliefs.

Dealing with Dependency

Parents of teens often have trouble letting go of the dependency that characterizes the parent-child relationship in their early years. Many parents have made caring for their children their primary preoccupation in life, their *job*. As adolescents naturally begin to desire more independence, these parents often feel as if they are losing their job, rather than evolving their job to meet new responsibilities. To ensure that they do not lose their familiar way of relating to their children, they over-function for their teens and take it upon themselves to solve the teen's problems, regulate the teen's emotions, and even plan the teen's future. This is the *modus operandi* of "helicopter parenting," in which parents constantly hover over every detail of their child's life, ready to fix problems, give advice, and swoop in to rescue them, if needed.

In many cases, the pattern of over-functioning by parents is established during the teen's early years. When children struggle academically or socially, for example, parents may take it upon themselves to *prop*

Mission: Control

Theodore was a creative 17-year-old boy, a talented guitarist, songwriter, and frontman for a rock band he and some friends formed this past year. Theodore's parents sent him to a wilderness program because conflicts at home were leading to violence between the teen and his dad. Theodore was also using drugs extensively, and in the past year, he had experimented with just about every street drug available. Theodore particularly liked cocaine, and he bragged that it made him feel powerful.

In our first session, Theodore told me about his struggles with his father, a successful entrepreneur who placed high expectations on Theodore. He demanded that Theodore maintain at least a 3.5 GPA so he could get into a top college. He scrutinized Theodore's friends and made negative comments about those whom he thought were unsuitable. He even tried to control Theodore's guitar-playing by arranging for him to take lessons from an acclaimed guitarist in their town, then becoming very angry if Theodore did not practice daily. "I get you the best teacher around, and you can't even discipline yourself enough to practice regularly," his father would gripe.

According to Theodore, he and his father often fought over Theodore's refusal to attend church where his father was a deacon. Theodore described how angry and threatening his father would become when his son disagreed with his religious views. I got a taste of this in his father's letters to him in the wilderness, which were filled with Bible verses. When I asked him how he felt about that, Theodore shrugged his shoulders.

"He hates it that I don't believe in the same thing that he does," he said. "He tries to control everything. I've been dealing with that all of my life."

I realized then that this father's narcissism was alienating his son, who was willing to go to dangerous lengths to assert his identity as separate from his dad.

the child up by organizing tasks, guiding the child's work, and sometimes even doing the work for the child. The child, in turn, may not develop a sense of efficacy for meeting daily challenges. Instead, the child remains dependent on the over-functioning parent to handle his responsibilities. And, while these parents may feel conflicted about doing so many things for their children, they often strongly identify with that role. Over-functioning on behalf of a child also allows parents to avoid conflicts that might occur if they handed him more responsibility.

What I find among the parents with whom I work is that "propping up" has become a general approach to parenting, not a specific intervention to assist the teen with a particular issue. These parents tend to over-function for their teens because it makes them feel less anxious if they don't have to watch their child struggle.

A hallmark of healthy, mature relationships is what family therapists refer to as *differentiation of self*. Differentiation of self is the extent to which an individual can maintain self-integrity in the face of covert and overt pressure from others to think, feel, or act in certain ways. In other words, can you and your child maintain a sense of closeness and respect for each other while having different feelings, beliefs, or needs? To what extent do you and your child feel as if you must adjust your feelings, beliefs and needs to match those of family, friends, and colleagues, or conversely, get theirs to fit yours? If your child is anxious, do you feel a responsibility to manage the child's anxiety? Or do you put pressure on the child to stop feeling so anxious so that you won't have to feel anxious yourself?

A well-differentiated person is able to tolerate and even appreciate another person's feelings, beliefs and needs while maintaining a healthy connection with their own. A poorly differentiated person feels a high level of confusion and anxiety when faced with someone with different feelings, beliefs or needs. Consequently, they may feel bound to change themselves to keep peace, or they may feel driven to make the other person change what they feel, believe, or need in order to feel less discomfort.

Parents with tendencies toward narcissistic or dependent parenting often possess a low level of self-differentiation, which can typically be traced back to their experiences within their family-of-origin. If this sounds familiar, I encourage you to explore it further with a therapist, as well as with your child's treatment team. You may find that the process of differentiating is one of the most liberating and transformative experiences you can undertake. Without a doubt, engaging in the process of differentiating may allow you to take all of your relationships to a new level of authenticity and closeness.

Effective Self-Regulation

As teens are learning how to manage strong emotions and impulses, they depend on the important adults in their lives to offer guidance by example. Unfortunately, their parents are often not the best role models. Many of the families that I work with have become locked into a dynamic of poorly differentiated, emotional reactivity, where tempers flare and threats are hurled in reaction to each other's actions, beliefs, or feelings. Certainly, I understand how emotionally charged the family environment can become when there is a defiant or willful child. Yet, as a parent, it is very important that you recognize that your task is to help your child learn how to regulate his emotions and impulses, effectively and maturely. When he sees you fly off the handle, or hears you say cruel and mean things in a moment of frustration, you are modeling a poor example of self-regulation. Certainly, an occasional outburst or episode of reactivity is quite

Questions to Ponder on Narcissism and Dependency

- What do you imagine your child sees reflected in your responses to him or her?

- What do you see when you look at your child? What are his or her unique gifts, characteristics?

- What things about your child bother you the most? Why?

- How do you communicate acceptance to your child? Disapproval?

- What have you modeled for your child in terms of concern for how your behavior impacts others?

- In what ways have you propped up your child, rather than allowing him or her to struggle?

- What do you imagine your child sees reflected in your responses to him or her?

normal and expected. But, a pattern of emotional outbursts can have a detrimental impact on the relationship you have with your child, and obviously, it does not model a mature way of managing strong emotions.

Often when teens are experiencing intense emotions, they look to their environment for cues as to how to regulate these feelings. Researchers studying the brain have helped us understand that the adolescent brain is undergoing tremendous and critical developmental processes, whereby neural pathways are forming that regulate emotional life.[3] It's clear, then, that teens need assistance in understanding and regulating their emotions. Moreover, assistance from significant others actually contributes to how the brain becomes wired to manage emotions and impulses. For example, when teens experience frustration, they may lack the neural pathways that allow them to correctly identify their emotional state as one of frustration. What's more, they may not understand that frustration is a valid response to certain experiences, nor do they have confidence that they can tolerate frustration until they "cool down" and deal with whatever is frustrating them. As a result, teens will often look to others for ideas on how to tolerate frustration in mature and effective ways. Obviously, who they look to for assistance can directly affect their ability to manage future experiences of frustration.

When a child's emotional state is met by an emotionally reactive parental response, the child does not learn to effectively manage her own emotional experience. Instead, she comes to think that emotional experiences can trigger unpleasant outbursts, and, consequently, she may anxiously avoid emotional expression until she simply cannot contain it anymore. Then, as many of you know, a crisis ensues, often accompanied by hurled threats or objects and, sometimes, even physical altercations or meltdowns.

I commonly observe self-regulating problems in parents with whom I work. These issues are most often manifested as:

- Intense anxiety about the teen, especially about the teen's struggles;
- Reactivity to the teen's emotions, or inability to regulate their emotions in the presence of the teen's emotional expressions;
- Unpredictable response patterns, at times, calm in the face of stress, at other times displaying escalated responses of anger, anxiety, sadness;
- Disengagement from their emotions and those of others, such that emotional connections are difficult to maintain.

Questions to Ponder on Goal-Oriented Behavior

- What behaviors do you model for your child in terms of tolerating frustration while working towards a goal?

- How do you handle your child's frustration in working towards a goal? Do you rescue him? Do you do the work for him, shame him, or offer support?

Learning how to regulate your own emotional experience allows you to assist your child in doing the same. If you have a problem effectively regulating your emotions, I believe it is absolutely imperative that you seek help from a therapist.

Modeling Goal-Oriented Behavior

Does your teen observe in you the ability to delay gratification and to work diligently towards some goal? Or, does your teen see in you a low tolerance for solving frustrating problems and a tendency to pursue immediate gratification of your impulses, wants, and needs? Have you modeled for your teenager the process of working towards a goal? For example, has your teen seen you save and budget money for future purchases, or do you model an approach that suggests money grows on trees?

Most effective adults have developed an understanding that the future is connected to the present in a logical, sequential manner. Some of us have learned these things through our own enrollment in the school of hard knocks, or Reality 101. But, how do you handle it when your child needs to tolerate frustration while working hard towards a goal? Some parents do not manage this experience well, choosing instead to avoid potential conflict and keep the peace by doing the work for the child. Other parents want to spare their child (and themselves) the struggle.

So why is this a bad idea? Because to develop a healthy capacity to tolerate frustration, one must have frustrating experiences! When you, as parents, accept that it's important for teens to experience frustration so that they can learn to solve difficult problems with confidence, you will begin to see that frustrating experiences are opportunities for important growth. For many of you, having your child in a therapeutic school or program may provide just such opportunities for you and your child. The processes of working diligently to complete a therapeutic program, of maintaining your resolve to accomplish each step in the process, and of enduring the range of emotions that you will encounter along the way, all represent significant learning opportunities for parents and teens in therapeutic schools. As I discussed in chapter five, parental resolve to hold fast and stay the course in this process allows a teen to get on with their work in the therapeutic program. Thus, they learn important lessons about personal responsibility, about moving towards a goal through the choices they make, and about the rewards of sustained effort.

Your Parenting Style

There is a billboard you may have seen that reads: *The bus driver knows who your kid has a crush on…do you?* The blunt message of this billboard transmits a core truth: It is imperative that parents know their children, know what they are doing, what they are interested in, and who they are hanging out with. Often, by the time teens and their parents reach the point of seeking an intervention from a residential therapeutic program or school, their relationship is quite tense, and they lack feelings of close-

Questions to Ponder on Relating to Your Teen

▤ How would you describe your current relationship with your teen?

▤ Do you both feel a sense of closeness and mutual respect for one another?

○ Yes ○ No ○ Sometimes

▤ Do you and your child spend time together most days?

○ Yes ○ No ○ Sometimes

▤ Do you and your child lead lives that are somewhat disconnected, or are you estranged from each other?

○ Yes ○ No ○ Sometimes

▤ Do you feel like you really *know* your child and what his or her interests are?

○ Yes ○ No ○ Sometimes

▤ Do you know your child's friends?

○ Yes ○ No ○ Sometimes

▤ Does your child *feel known* by you?

○ Yes ○ No ○ Sometimes

▤ Does your child trust you?

○ Yes ○ No ○ Sometimes

▤ Does your child believe you give him or her enough space and acceptance to develop his or her individuality?

○ Yes ○ No ○ Sometimes

▤ Would your child say that your supervision and limits are too intrusive?

○ Yes ○ No ○ Sometimes

▤ Would your child complain that you are disengaged and that bad behavior or emotional outbursts get your attention?

○ Yes ○ No ○ Sometimes

▤ Do you have a relationship with your child that is characterized by angry dependency?

○ Yes ○ No ○ Sometimes

▤ Are you and your child emotionally reactive to each other?

○ Yes ○ No ○ Sometimes

▤ Are there hurts or resentments that you and your child need to be work through and repair?

○ Yes ○ No ○ Sometimes

▤ Is there a pattern of inconsistency in your availability to your child?

○ Yes ○ No ○ Sometimes

ness and connection. Many times, the relationship's foundation of trust has been ruptured, and both sides have been hurt in significant ways. As we focus on identifying what you should be working on while your child is away, I believe it is essential to take a good look at the state of the relationship between you and your teen.

In chapter two, I described to you how psychosocial development occurs within the context of significant relationships over time. The parent-child relationship is especially important in this developmental process. It is, after all, the first relationship that the child experiences, and as such, is one of the most formative in terms of the child's emerging sense of self and relationships. Likewise, it is usually within the parent-child relationship that children have opportunities to grow and get ready to be launched into young adulthood.

The parent-child relationship must go through various evolutions over time. An infant's utter dependency on the parents gives way to curious explorations of the world and a growing sense of independence during toddlerhood. Later, school-aged children will spend more time away from home, engaged in academic endeavors under the supervision of teachers; yet, parents will remain the guardians of their welfare, responsible for being attentive to their children's adjustment to school and peer relationships and to their development of self-confidence and self-esteem. During adolescence, the relationship shifts again, becoming a struggle at times, as teens vacillate between identifying themselves *with* their parents and identifying themselves *against* them.

In childhood, parents' *accurate attunement* to their children's feelings, beliefs, and needs as they change and develop helps them feel truly accepted, known and loved. Children develop a healthy self-perception based on the accurate reflections of attuned parents. At the same time, parents should be providing *appropriate containment* for their children, supervising them, setting appropriate boundaries, and limiting their child's experience, based on knowledge of what they are and are not capable of handling. When accurate attunement and appropriate containment are applied consistently over time, children develop a clear sense of who they are and what they are capable of, as well as an understanding of their appropriate boundaries. They also begin to learn how to relate to others with self-confidence and concern for their welfare.

As you reflect on these and other questions, I encourage you to journal your thoughts and feelings. Certainly, these can be topics of exploration in your own therapy. Perhaps, at the appropriate time, these can be topics for conversation between you and your teen while he is engaged in a therapeutic program or school. I believe it is very important that you begin a new dialogue with your teen about your relationship. Your therapist or treatment team can certainly help with this. In fact, therapeutic schools and programs often facilitate conversations between parents and teens to help each of them to engage honestly and effectively, using healthy communication skills.

Problems with Accurate Attunement or Appropriate Containment

I also encourage you to reflect upon how well you provide accurate attunement and containment to your child. Do you struggle to find the

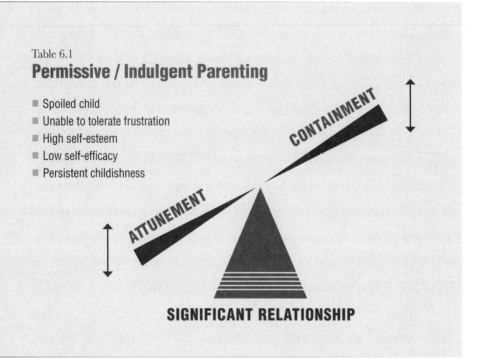

Table 6.1

Permissive / Indulgent Parenting

- Spoiled child
- Unable to tolerate frustration
- High self-esteem
- Low self-efficacy
- Persistent childishness

CONTAINMENT

ATTUNEMENT

SIGNIFICANT RELATIONSHIP

appropriate balance of these dimensions in your relationship with your teen? It may be helpful to think of attunement and containment as being in dialectical tension. What this means is that they are at opposite ends of a spectrum, and as such, are always connected. I like to use the analogy of a teeter-totter to illustrate this dialectical tension.

The fulcrum of the teeter-totter is the parenting relationship. At one end of the teeter-totter is *accurate attunement* (what researchers identify as parental responsiveness, warmth, or supportiveness), at the other end is *appropriate containment* (what researchers identify as parental demands or control). Ideally, we are seeking to balance the teeter-totter. Supervision and limit-setting, which are the actions of containment and parental control, are intimately connected to the parent's availability and attentive awareness to the child's needs and feelings, which are the actions of accurate attunement. However, what I observe in many of the families with whom I meet is imbalance in these two dimensions, such that the teeter-totter is weighted down on one side.

When the teeter-totter is imbalanced because of too much attunement and not enough containment, you often see kids who are spoiled, feel entitled, and who believe rules and limits do not apply to them. This is probably the most common type of imbalance that I see in my work. Parents who focus on attunement are advocates of promoting their children's self-esteem and helping them feel good about themseleves. However, if these parents don't push their children to mature by limiting childish behavior, these kids do not develop the maturity that allows them to experience real success in the adolescent world. Thus, the self-esteem that has been so nourished by their parents begins to be eroded by their experience in the world of relationships, because these children are ill-equipped to solve the increasingly complex problems that they face.

Dr. Diana Baumrind, one of the most well-recognized and often-cited researchers of how parenting styles impact children's behavior, labels this parenting style as *permissive*. She describes permissive parents as being "more responsive than they are demanding. They are nontraditional and lenient, do not require mature behavior, allow considerable self-regulation, and avoid confrontation."[4] Baumrind observed that children of permissive parents tend to exhibit more problem behaviors and perform less well in school. However, they tend to have higher self-esteem, better social skills, and lower levels of depression than children whose parents have different parenting styles.

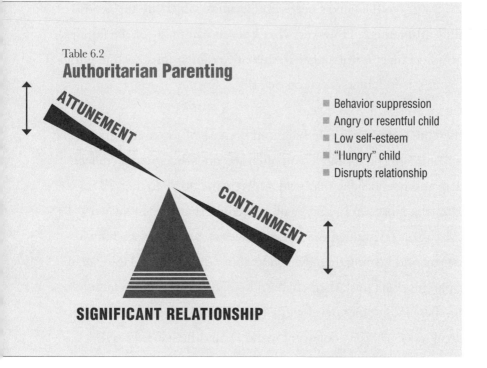

Table 6.2
Authoritarian Parenting

ATTUNEMENT

CONTAINMENT

- Behavior suppression
- Angry or resentful child
- Low self-esteem
- "Hungry" child
- Disrupts relationship

SIGNIFICANT RELATIONSHIP

At the other end of the continuum are those parents whose parenting style tends to be imbalanced by too much containment and too little attunement. Baumrind labeled this parenting style as *authoritarian*. These parents, according to Baumrind, "are obedience- and status-oriented, and expect their orders to be obeyed without explanation."[5] Children of these parents tend to perform well in school and are less likely to engage in drug abuse or antisocial behavior, but they are more likely to be unhappy, anxious, and withdrawn, and to demonstrate poor frustration tolerance.

Parents who strike a healthy balance between attunement and containment possess a parenting style that Baumrind labels *authoritative*. According to Baumrind, authoritative parents "monitor and impart clear standards for their children's conduct. They are assertive, but not intrusive and restrictive. Their disciplinary methods are supportive, rather than punitive. They want their children to be assertive as well as socially responsible, and self-regulated as well as cooperative."[6]

How would you label your parenting style? Perhaps you are very attuned to your teen's feelings and needs and feel very connected to her, but you struggle with setting limits. Or perhaps you provide inadequate supervision of your teen, giving her plenty of trust and space, perhaps more trust than she truly deserves and more space than she is ready to manage. It may be that your attunement to your teen has not evolved to match his developmental level. Thus, when he is anxious or frustrated, you are too quick to solve problems for him, rather than pushing him to learn how to solve his own problems.

I recall one boy in my care, whose father had died during his childhood. His mother explained to me that she knew her son was spoiled, but that she had been quite permissive due to her son's loss (and hers). There can be many valid explanations for why parents develop an imbalanced parenting approach, of course. Nonetheless, the challenge for parents is to strike a balance between attunement and setting limits, regardless of the circumstances.

Perhaps you are too rule-bound in your parenting. You may do a great job of setting limits and keeping abreast of what your child is up to, but you find that your child resents you and acts out in secretive ways to defy your control. Maybe your limit-setting has produced shame in your child, so that she believes that she is inherently bad whenever she breaks

Table 6.3
Authoritative Parenting

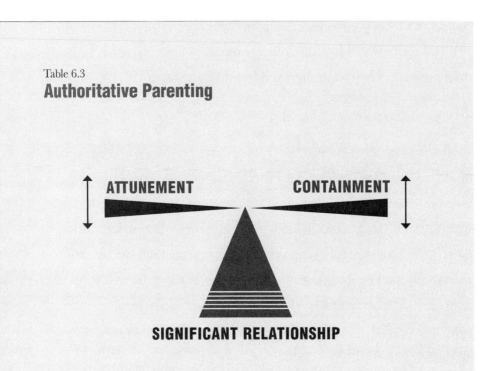

your rules. Or perhaps she anxiously avoids disappointing your expectations and demands, but feels restricted in her ability to exercise her curiosity, freely and enthusiastically. For parents like this, the goal is to develop greater attunement to and warmth for their child. Ironically, this often strengthens a child's willingness to follow a parent's expectations.

Regardless of where you fall on this continuum, I believe there is hope that you can learn new ways of interacting with your teen such that you can provide a better balance of attunement and containment.

Your Home Environment

Another very important topic for you to reflect upon is your home environment. Family therapists have helped us understand how profoundly

Questions to Ponder about Life at Home

■ Are there marital issues that need to be addressed?

○ Yes ○ No ○ Sometimes

■ Are you in the midst or the aftermath of a problematic divorce?

○ Yes ○ No

■ Are there communication issues that need to be addressed?

○ Yes ○ No ○ Sometimes

■ Do you bring a high level of stress home from your work environment?

○ Yes ○ No ○ Sometimes

■ Does your family have fun together, laugh and play together?

○ Yes ○ No ○ Sometimes

■ Do you eat meals together?

○ Yes ○ No ○ Sometimes

■ Are there traumatic incidents or other big problems in your family that are not talked about (e.g., experiences of abuse or abandonment; addictions; etc.)?

○ Yes ○ No

■ Or, is there too much talked about regarding certain issues (e.g., do the kids know too much about your marital difficulties)?

○ Yes ○ No ○ Sometimes

■ Are you connected to a community of friends and families who know your teen well?

○ Yes ○ No ○ Sometimes

■ Is your child being raised by a "village" of adults who know and supervise him and who he respects?

○ Yes ○ No ○ Sometimes

interconnected families are. To be sure, no person in a family is an island. Family systems theory tells us that the behavior of each member within a family not only impacts the behavior of other members, but is often supported and enabled by them. Thus, while family members may complain about or punish one member's problematic behavior, the reality is that their behavior may actually be promoting the problematic behavior. With this in mind, I often refer to the teens in my care as "symptom-bearers" for their family. In other words, because their problems generally are the primary focus of family members, they often serve to keep the attention off of other family issues or processes that need to be addressed.

Creating a Coherent Narrative of your Life

Attachment researcher Dr. Mary Main and her colleagues developed an instrument, the Adult Attachment Interview (AAI), to better understand how aspects of a parents' own childhood history affect the way they act towards their children.[7] What they discovered gave credence to what many of us already thought. In fact, a parent's childhood experiences do impact his or her parenting behavior, but in ways that many of us had not considered. What Main and her colleagues discovered was that *how* parents made sense of their childhood was the most important predictor of their attachment behavior with their own children. Those who were able to create a coherent narrative about their lives, regardless of their circumstances, were able to achieve secure adult attachment status, and, therefore, were able to bond with their children in a healthy manner.[8]

What is meant by a "coherent narrative?" According to Siegel, a coherent life story is one that integrates various dimensions of personal experience into an accurate, clear and full account.[9] In other words, it is a sensitive and reflective telling of one's experiences, incorporating the realms of emotion, thought, body sensations, and behavior, and describing them in the context of relationships with significant others and the momentous events of one's life. This deeply integrated self-understanding appears to facilitate one's ability to be more attuned and empathic in present relationships. Siegel believes that practicing mindfulness facilitates greater coherence in our personal narratives because mindfulness

Questions for Parental Self-Reflection

■ What was it like growing up? Who was in your family?

■ How did you get along with your parents early in your childhood? How did the relationship evolve throughout your youth and up until the present time?

■ How did your relationship with your mother and father differ and how were they similar? Are there ways in which you try to be like, or try not to be like, each of your parents?

■ Did you ever feel rejected or threatened by your parents? Were there other experiences you had that felt overwhelming or traumatizing in your life, during childhood or beyond? Do any of these experiences still feel very much alive? Do they continue to influence your life?

■ How did your parents discipline you as a child? What impact did that have on your childhood, and how do you feel it affects your role as a parent now?

■ Do you recall your earliest separations from your parents? What was it like? Did you ever have prolonged separations from your parents?

■ Did anyone significant in your life die during your childhood, or later in your life? What was that like for you at the time, and how does that loss affect you now?

■ How did your parents communicate with you when you were happy and excited? Did they join with you in your enthusiasm? When you were distressed or unhappy as a child, what would happen? Did your father and mother respond differently to you during these emotional times? How?

■ Was there anyone else besides your parents in your childhood who took care of you? What was that relationship like for you? What happened to these individuals? What is it like for you when you let others take care of your child now?

■ If you had difficult times during your childhood, were there positive relationships in or outside of your home that you could depend on during those times? How do you feel those connections benefited you then, and how might they help you now?

■ How have your childhood experiences influenced your relationships with others as an adult? Do you find yourself trying not to behave in certain ways because of what happened to you as a child? Do you have patterns of behavior that you'd like to alter but have difficulty changing?

■ What impact do you think your childhood has had on your adult life in general, including the ways in which you think of yourself and the ways you relate to your children? What would you like to change about the way you understand yourself and relate to others?

develops the skill of reflective awareness of one's experience.[10]

An incoherent narrative, on the other hand, fails to integrate important dimensions of our personal experience. For example, one parent described how his father never attended any of his sporting events, even though he had been an exceptionally talented athlete who received offers to play college baseball. "I always knew he loved me, though," he said. Interestingly, at the time, this parent and I were discussing his relationship with his teenaged daughter, who had lamented the fact that her dad had never come to a concert by the rock band she had formed. Obviously, his inability to integrate his disappointment and sadness about his father not seeing him play baseball prevented him from being accurately attuned to the importance of his presence at his daughter's concerts.

Do you have a coherent narrative for your life? Have you reflected on your experiences as a child and teenager and made sense of them so that they tell a full and complete story? Are you in therapy yourself? I cannot emphasize to you enough how important parental therapy appears to be in terms of building a new and healthy relationship with your struggling teen. Some therapeutic schools and programs go so far as to insist that parents engage in their own therapy while their kids are enrolled in the program.

There are often a number of reasons why parents do not seek therapy for themselves, not the least of which are time and financial constraints. However, when you invest in deepening your understanding of yourself and your life experiences, you are laying the groundwork that will allow you to be more effective in providing the attunement and containment your teen needs from you if he is to move forward in his development.

[1] Hair, H.J. "Outcomes for children and adolescents after residential treatment: A review of research from 1993 to 2003." *Journal of Child and Family Studies*, no. 14. (2005): 551-575.

[2] Levine, M. *The Price of Privilege: How parental pressure and material advantage are creating a generation of disconnected and unhappy kids.* (New York: Harper Collins, 2006).

[3] Siegel, D.J. The Developing Mind: How relationships and the brain interanct to shape who we are. (New York: Guilford, 1999).

[4] Baumrind, D. "The influence of parenting style on adolescent competence and substance use." *Journal of Early Adolescence*, no. 1 (1991): 62.

[5] Baumrind, 62.

[6] Baumrind, 62.

[7] Main, M. "The Adult Attachment Interview: Fear, Attention, Safety, and Discourse Processes." Journal of the American Psychoanalytic Association, no. 4 (2000) 1055-1096.

[8] Siegel, D.J. and M. Hartzell. Parenting from the Inside Out: How a Deeper Self-Understanding Can Help You Raise Children Who Thrive. (New York: Penguin, 2003).

[9] Siegel, D.J. (1999)

[10] Siegel, D.J. *The Mindful Brain: Reflection and Attunement in the Cultivation of Well-Being* (New York: Norton, 2007).

11 Siegel, D.J. and M. Hartzell (2003) 133-134.

CHAPTER SEVEN

COMING HOME

How can you support teens in the real world?

Therapeutic schools and programs have proliferated in the last 10–15 years to meet a crucial need for struggling teens and their families. As I discussed in chapter one, the symptom-based treatment approach of child and adolescent psychiatry, coupled with the serious limitations of outpatient therapy, have left many parents scratching their heads as they watch their teens exhibit ever more dysfunctional and even dangerous behavior patterns.

Symptom-based approaches have merit, to be sure, and the research used by managed-care companies to determine which treatment methods they will approve and reimburse confirms their efficacy. However, many of the troubling symptoms that teens are exhibiting appear to be rooted in and maintained by the cultural reality in which they dwell. Today, the distractions available for children and teens are innumerable. Worse, with so many activities to plug into, many young people are missing out on real-time connections with attuned parents and adults. Drugs are so widely available that many children reach adolescence having already tried marijuana, alcohol, and cigarettes. Then there are the examples set by popular icons. Hip-hop artists promote brazen egocentrism, glorify drug abuse, and objectify females. Many teens are not yet able to approach such material with mature moral judgment. And, standing in the wings of these teen dramas are parents, many of whom have lost their authority over their children and who lack connections with other parents who can support them in holding limits, providing structure, and supervising teens.

A number of therapeutic schools and programs provide excellent clinical treatment to teens who have fallen through the cracks or who are on bleak behavioral trajectories. Many of these programs are armed to the hilt with sophisticated clinical expertise, enabling them to remediate many of the problems that struggling teens present. But, ultimately, what makes these programs therapeutic is that they provide a structured community that not only limits distractions and drugs, but engages teens in deep and significant relationships with attuned adults and with adult-directed peer groups, who support the development of psychological maturity among their members. The fruit of these communities is seen in the adolescents who come out of these schools with:

- An understanding that their present decisions and behavior directly influence their future goals, both academic and personal;
- The knowledge that they are part of various communities, beginning with their family and broadening to include their circle of friends and society at large;
- The belief that they have responsibilities and obligations as a member of these groups; and
- New skills that will help them to manage their impulses and emotions more effectively, such that they are able to make better decisions.

As these teens begin to flourish outside of their therapeutic schools, however, they must still endure the normal tides of adolescent life. But, it appears that those who attend therapeutic schools and programs are better prepared than many of their peers to ride the waves of adolescence and young adulthood. What's more, they appear to be more aware of and wary of the waves that can drag them down or undermine their relationships.

Creating a "More-Real World"

Parents often worry that therapeutic schools and programs do not adequately prepare teens to live in the *real world*. In speaking with many of my colleagues, and through my own observations of struggling teens, I've come to a different conclusion. When I look at teen problems through the lens of development, I see that the so-called *real world* actually possesses some very *unreal* features and challenges for many teens. If the goal for adolescence is to develop an approach to the world that will enable them to succeed as adults, and if this goal is accomplished through significant relationships that both support and challenge teens in their development, then a growing number of adolescents actually are not having the *real* experiences that they need in the *real world*. In fact, many are getting derailed in their development because of their childish approaches to relationships and real-life problems. Unless changes are made in mainstream America, too many of our teens are poised to continue struggling as adults.

As I mentioned earlier, my hope for this book was twofold: First, I want to support parents in the process of enrolling their child in a therapeutic program or school; and, second, I want to challenge parents to begin transforming themselves, so that they will be better prepared to parent their teens upon returning home. Throughout history, when people leave the mainstream to go into the wilderness or desert to experience transformation, the challenge is always to bring back wisdom gained and to share it for the benefit of civilization. So, whether you are just beginning the process of enrolling your teen in a therapeutic program or are at the end of this process, I want to challenge you to find ways that you can help create a *more-real world* for families of children and teens.

Perhaps our worry about how teens in therapeutic programs will transition back to the real world highlight the need for some real-world revisions in parenting and teen culture. I don't mean to sound reactionary, but I am very concerned about the level of immaturity in so many of the teens that I see, a problem that is made worse by the lack of attuned adults available to supervise them as they move through a minefield of challenges to their development.

I am especially concerned about the prevalence and intensity of teen alcohol and drug use. We are not simply talking about a little alcohol or a little marijuana. Instead, it's becoming commonplace for teens to engage in binge drinking and to have cocaine, crack, ecstasy, LSD, methamphetamine, and heroin readily available to them. In addition, prescription medications are being used extensively; in fact, the very same drugs prescribed to teens to treat symptoms of poor concentration and hyperactivity are being used recreationally. Because so many teens lack mature judgment about the impact of using drugs and also have little supervision from attuned adults, many are vulnerable to making very poor, very risky decisions, especially if they are already struggling in other areas of their lives. And, the peer group of "cool teens" is heavily influenced by the endless array of media images they are plugged into, many of which promote drug and alcohol use. In fact, many of these images have become prevalent on mainstream television, in mainstream music, and in movies that reach the masses.

After years of watching teens who were on a developmental collision course in mainstream America make significant psychological improvements in a structured, therapeutic environment, I believe we need to begin transforming our communities so that we are more attuned to and present for our teens. I'd like to share my thoughts about how we can make this happen in hopes that it will inspire your thinking about these matters. I believe we are approaching a crossroads in our cultural understanding and treatment of adolescents, given that so many appear to be slipping off track during their teen years. Those of you who have struggled with your teen and have seen how they can flourish in a residential therapeutic program are well-positioned to begin raising public awareness about the attitudes and practices within our culture that simply are not in the best interests of our children and teens. Perhaps you can become a witness to other parents within your communities about the benefits of nurturing and protecting parent-teen relationships by being accurately attuned to their needs, feelings, opinions and actions and of providing appropriate containment and supervision. Instead of being a symptom-bearer of our culture's dysfunctional beliefs about parenting teenagers, you can become a healer and a voice of experience within your sphere of influence.

How do we begin to transform our culture? I grant you, it won't be easy. Changing cultural values, assumptions, and practices requires time, resources, and sustained effort. Yet, I do not underestimate the power of individuals to become agents of change within their segments of the broader society. And, as more parents see how therapeutic programs facilitate healthy development in their teens, more of them will be able to speak with authority to other parents in their communities about how we can create a better environment for raising our teens.

Mentoring

If you are like most parents of troubled teens, you've probably had times when you felt as if you'd failed as a parent. You may have doubted your instincts, questioned your competence, and blamed yourself for your teen's difficulties. Thus, the idea of becoming a mentor to other parents of adolescents may seem like quite a stretch. Yet, you are or have been involved in a crucial process with your teen, one which has increased your understanding and given you invaluable wisdom about parenting teenagers in today's world. In other words, you may be exactly the kind of mentor other parents can trust. You've been there, done that.

Perhaps the obvious place for you to start mentoring other families is through your child's therapeutic school or program. Many therapeutic programs are looking to connect new parents with those who are further along in the process. This could be a wonderful opportunity for you to support other parents who are enduring the emotional process that goes along with sending your child away to a therapeutic program. It can also validate your own experience. But, more importantly, mentoring con-nects you to a community of parents who are growing in their under-standing of how teens' difficulties develop, and they are intentionally changing how they parent their children.

Over the years, I have found that some of the most meaningful experiences for parents of teens in therapeutic programs are the workshops and seminars that bring parents together. What I have heard from parents time and time again is how wonderful it is to hear that other parents have actually had similar experiences with their teens. They also report feeling a sense of hope when they speak to parents whose kids have actually improved during the process, and who report feeling a deeper sense of connection with their teens. Often, conversations that begin by sharing stories about the challenges of parenting their teens lead to discussions about the obstacles facing parents in today's world. As these conversations continue, consensus often develops among parents about the importance of regaining an authoritative presence in their teens' lives. Joining together to support and encourage each other in effective parenting is precisely the kind of community model for parenting that our contemporary culture so desperately needs.

Parental Networking

Effective therapeutic schools and programs link parents together, while providing clear structure and guidance to help parents set limits for their teens and interact appropriately with them. Parents discover that by following the program's rules and expectations, they are actually supporting other parents in doing the same thing. Refusing to follow program expectations makes the job of other parents more difficult. Being joined together for a shared purpose—raising mature, well-adjusted teenagers—strengthens a parent's ability to set and uphold appropriate limits. It is the lack of a shared community understanding for making appropriate parental decisions that is one of the major barriers parents in the *real* world face. I wonder what it would take in order to develop networks of parents who are mutually committed to holding certain expectations among their teens.

Certainly, a community-based model for parenting used to be more prevalent in our towns and villages. As we have become increasingly alienated from our neighbors and more individualized, we have lost a unified approach to parenting. I don't believe it is critical that parents all use the same model for parenting, but it is important that parents communicate with each other, share ideas, and support each other in the job of raising children into effective and mature adults. Being connected to each other is key.

I encourage parents who have had the experience of being in a cohesive community structure such as a therapeutic school to reach out to other parents in their home communities. Ask questions of each other, exchange ideas about parenting, and ask other parents to support the holding of limits. Build relationships with other parents and share what you have learned. Obviously, there will always be those parents who refuse to confront their teen's behavior and may even support misbehavior by their teen. However, I believe most parents really want to do the right thing, they just don't always know how to go about it. In many instances, parents look to see what other parents are doing before making parenting decisions. I believe a greater connection among parents would empower some to uphold limits for their teens that are more effective. Reaching out to parents in your neighborhood and schools is a good place to start networking. Encouraging therapists or school counselors to support information sessions or parenting seminars might also be useful. And, establishing support networks via the Internet can draw in parents who might otherwise be excluded.

Becoming a Voice for Change

Mothers Against Drunk Driving (MADD) is an excellent example of parents who came together around a specific concern. This group has raised public awareness of the serious impact of drunk driving on families by sharing moving and personal accounts of losing a child in an accident caused by an intoxicated driver. MADD has also become a vocal presence in national and local political arenas, and it has had a tremendous influence in legislation and law enforcement. It has become a support group for families of victims, and it has provided educational resources to schools, colleges, and community groups.

I believe the time is ripe for parents of struggling teens to form alliances to raise awareness of how difficult it is in contemporary America to raise children into mature adults. Many parents of troubled teens know first-hand the limitations of current treatment approaches. I encourage these parents to become activists in challenging the reimbursement policies of managed-care insurance companies that limit support for families whose children have not benefited from the approved outpatient treatments.

The parents I work with understand how technology and contemporary media are creating barriers to effective parenting. They know that their teen's entitlement and disconnection is fueled by being always plugged in to a technological distraction. These parents also recognize how the lack of connection among parents and the lack of a cohesive community model for parenting interferes with their ability to identify appropriate limits for their teens, and to follow through in setting and enforcing these limits. As I have echoed throughout this book, parents of teens who are struggling are not alone, though many of them feel alone. I challenge parents who have gone through the experience of having to send their teen away to a therapeutic program or school to become an active voice in discussing the concerns listed above, as well as many other concerns that I am sure I have missed.

Being Available and Attentive to Teens

The most essential variable in terms of helping children grow into mature adults is the presence of significant relationships with adults who are available and attentive to their experiences. I encourage parents of teens who are involved in therapeutic programs and schools to be present and attentive in the lives of their teens and their teen's peers. I am convinced that too many teens today are allowed to roam the World Wide Web, to interact with peers through instant-messaging and text-messaging, and to create profiles on MySpace or FaceBook outside of the supervision and knowledge of their parents. This secretive nature of many of their lives extends to the world of their peers, where many are engaging in substance abuse and other risky behaviors without their parents' knowledge.

I fully understand that teens are in the process of separating from their parents and assuming more autonomy. I believe it is important that adults support this process. But, the reality is that we live in a very different world than any previous generation has known. I believe it is imperative in today's world that parents are vigilant in supervising their teens. A new kind of parental presence is called for, one that is characterized by flexibility and willingness to grow and evolve along with the child.

I've emphasized in earlier chapters how important it is that adults are accurately attuned to their children, that they are attentive and responsive to their needs, beliefs, and feelings. At the same time, parents must contain their teen's experience through setting limits and providing supervision, so that teens can adequately benefit from and make sense of the world around them. To provide this kind of relationship for teens, parents must reflect upon their lives and develop accurate, coherent narratives of their experiences. Parenting challenges us to face ourselves more honestly and to confront our culture, as well. If we are to grow as parents and launch children into young adulthood with a level of maturity that enables them to manage their lives and relationships effectively, we must be willing to undertake this hard work.

AFTERWORD

RELATIONSHIPS RESTORED

I recently spoke with Jason and Leah, the couple you met in the introduction of this book. It had been almost a year since we'd met to discuss their daughter, Sylvia, and I was interested to receive an update on how they were all faring. I immediately noted how relaxed the two of them appeared in this meeting—a far cry from where they were when I first met them.

The three of us recounted our time together when Sylvia was in wilderness. We laughed at how angry and obstinate she had been, and Leah recalled how little she and Jason slept during that time.

"It's only been in the last four months or so that I've really been able to sleep through the night, knowing that Sylvia is okay," Leah told me. Jason nodded, adding that it is a welcome luxury to go to bed at night knowing that their daughter is happy and taken care of.

Leah told me that she had recently re-read the letters they had received from Sylvia while she was in wilderness. "Although it was really hard to read some of those again, particularly the angry manipulative ones, I can now see that Sylvia was beginning to find her voice with us through that experience."

Jason agreed: "Yeah, she used to say that we never listened to her, that we were never satisfied with her, that we didn't understand her. You know, we wanted to understand her, but I don't think we really did back then. There was just too much shouting and conflict, and we were terrified at the choices she was making and the kids she was hanging around with. None of those kids, by the way, have ever stopped by to check on Sylvia or ask how she is doing."

"It was while she was at wilderness that she first began to talk about her feelings," says Leah. "And, although it was hard to hear some of her feelings about me, it actually made us closer."

After Sylvia completed the wilderness program, she went on to a therapeutic boarding school in the west. I remembered how difficult it was for Jason and Leah to send her to a long-term program, and asked how things had gone there so far.

"It was a rough start," Jason admitted. "Leah and I were still struggling with whether or not it was the right decision, Sylvia wanted to be back in her old school, and it took us awhile to get used to the new rules and structure of the program. We really like her therapist, though, and it was good for us to hear how invested she is in Sylvia's growth. She really seems to get it."

"Yeah," Leah agreed. "She's been great. And Sylvia has started to do so well in school. She loves her teachers, and last term she received an award for academic excellence from her physics teacher. I can't believe it, really! She also loves the friends she has met at the school. It was really funny, but last time we visited her, we got to take her off campus for a couple of days. We had a great time together, but she just kept talking about how much she loves the kids at the school. On our last day of the visit, I started to cry about leaving her, and Sylvia got a little bit sad, but once she saw some of her friends, she quickly joined them and started laughing and talking with them. It's been so long since I've seen her that happy and connected to her friends."

"I guess the biggest change that we've seen is that Sylvia seems much more confident in herself," Jason reported. "She has gotten really good at talking about her feelings, better than either of her parents, really, and she seems to be thinking more realistically about how she wants to do well on her SATs so she can go to college after she graduates. She also doesn't try to manipulate us like she used to. If we say 'no' to something, she might get a bit frustrated, but she lets it go."

Jason and Leah went on to tell me that Sylvia would soon be eligible to have her first visit home, and they were both excited and nervous about that. "We've already been talking with Sylvia and her therapist about some ground rules for that," Leah said. "Hopefully, it will go well. I think it will."

"I'm really happy for all of you," I told the two of them. "So, overall, do you think this has been a good decision?"

Both of them nodded, and Leah spoke up: "It's been incredibly diffi-cult not having her home for so long. I've missed her terribly, but I know this has helped her and us to get to a better place. I actually feel closer to her now than I have for years, and it's incredible to see her doing so well and feeling so good about herself. And Jason and I have learned a lot about ourselves through this process; so we've grown, too. It scares me to think where we might have been if we had not done this."

Paul Wesley Case, Psy.D received his B.A. in English from Millsaps College in 1991, his Master's in Clinical Psychology from Wheaton College in 1996, and his Doctorate in Clinical Psychology from Wheaton College in 2000. He completed his post-doctoral work at the Montana State Hospital, where he spearheaded the development and implementation of treatment pathways for hospital patients.

Paul then took a position as Clinical Supervisor with Montana Academy, a therapeutic boarding school outside of Kalispell, Montana. There, Paul developed a passion and clinical focus for working with adolescents and their families. In 2006, Paul joined the clinical staff at Second Nature Blue Ridge Wilderness Program in Clayton, Georgia.

Paul's clinical interests include bereavement, trauma, cutting and self-harm, substance abuse, attachment struggles, oppositional behavior, emotional regulation, and developmental immaturity. Paul works primarily from a cognitive developmental orientation. At the heart of effective treatment with adolescents, he believes, is a relationship in which the adolescent feels that an adult "gets it" about him or her and, within that context, sets appropriate limits that promote growth and maturity.

Paul has presented papers at various conferences, including the annual conference of the American Psychological Association and the annual conference of the National Association of Therapeutic Schools and Programs.

Paul lives in the Atlanta area where he enjoys listening to and composing music, trying out new restaurants, and spending time with his family.